REA

ALLEN COUNTY PUBLIC LIBRARY

3 1833 00093 9063

428.4 P81g
Pope, Lillie.
Guidelines to teaching
remedial reading

D1572955

9.95

GUIDELINES TO
TEACHING
REMEDIAL
READING

Revised

✓

GUIDELINES TO
TEACHING

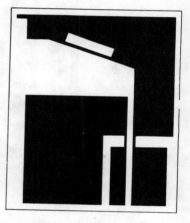

Revised

REMEDIAL READING

LILLIE POPE

BOOK LAB / NORTH BERGEN, NEW JERSEY

Designed and illustrated by Irv Glucksman
Cover design by Jerry Fargo

Library of Congress Catalogue Card No. 74-25232
Paperbound: ISBN 87594-119-2

© 1975, Lillie Pope, Brooklyn, New York
Second Edition

All rights reserved including the right to reproduce this
book, or any portion thereof, in any form except for
the inclusion of brief quotations in a review.

Published by BOOK-LAB
500 74th Street
North Bergen, New Jersey 07047

To Miriam and Deborah

Table of Contents

Part 2 / How to Teach

Part 3 / Additional Aids

Part 4 / Teaching Reading to Students to Whom English Is a Foreign Language

Part 5 / Useful Teaching Material

Introduction

There are, unfortunately, too many individuals handicapped by a lack of the formal educational skills of reading and arithmetic. To help these people, compensatory educational programs have been set up throughout the country. Most of these programs are outside of the established educational structure. They are housed in churches, stores, settlement houses, and schools. Many are part of larger anti-poverty programs.

Because the supply of trained remedial teachers is limited, tutors are employed in the reading programs. But tutors who lack adequate guidance may fail with their students just as the regular educational system has failed with them.

This manual for tutors deals with the specific techniques needed for teaching children, adolescents, and adults to read; it describes the problems of the student who comes for remedial instruction; it discusses the nature of the relationship between the tutor and the student; it outlines in simple terms the skills that are involved in the act of reading; it shows the tutor how to evaluate the student's reading level and determine his strengths and weaknesses. Finally, the tutor is guided in organizing an effective program of instruction and is provided with helpful tips and suggestions for materials useful in providing reading instruction in a program limited in funds.

Preface to The Second Edition

This book was originally written as a guide for tutors involved in compensatory educational programs. Experience has shown that the book may also be used advantageously by teachers for group or class instruction. In response to repeated requests, a new section has been added to guide the instructor of those for whom English is a second language.

I wish to thank Deborah Edel, Abraham Haklay and Belle Silverstone for their invaluable assistance and suggestions; and I thank my husband for his patience.

How to Use This Book

A. Before you meet your student

1. Read Part I carefully.

2. Skim through Parts II and III to acquaint yourself with the type of information available.

3. If your student has not yet learned to speak English, read Part IV.

B. After you meet your student

1. Determine his reading level. See pages 39-48.
   a. If he reads at the third grade level or below, see pages 51-69.
   b. If he reads at the fourth grade level or above, see pages 70-75.

2. Determine his reading requirements
   a. If he reads at the third grade level or below:
      Target skills are described on pages 86-89, 75.
      Suggestions for correcting bad reading habits, see pages 79-81.
      Applicable word lists, see pages 93-119, 122.
      Useful games, see pages 159-166, 175-177.
      Additional materials, see pages 111, 112, 167-173.
   b. If his reading level is fourth to eighth grade:
      Target skills are described on pages 86-89, 75.
      Suggestions for correcting bad reading habits, see pages 79-81.
      Applicable word lists, see pages 120-128.
      Useful games, see pages 159-166, 175-177.
      Additional materials, see pages 170-175.
   c. If he reads at the ninth grade level or above:
      Target skills are described on pages 86-89, 75.
      Suggestions for correcting bad reading habits, see pages 79-81.
      Word lists, see pages 159-166, 175-177.
      Additional materials, see pages 173-175.

3. Plan Your Instruction
      Sample lesson plan, see page 83.

PART 1

Before You Begin To Tutor

Before You Begin to Tutor

The most important tool for learning is reading. This manual concentrates on instruction in remedial reading and can therefore be used to assist a tutor participating in any type of remedial education program. Since you are giving your time and energy, you want to do a good job. You will therefore have to know your subject and your student; you will also have to know how to impart your knowledge to the student. The reasons for his failure are complex; you must assume that your student is not stupid and that he can learn. You must also remember that the teacher has no magic formulas; the teacher can help the student open the door to learning, but the student must walk through. Your confidence in his capability to create a fuller life for himself, your confidence that more rewarding job opportunities will be available to him, must be transmitted to him.

The student will have many doubts and hesitations. You must convince him that there is hope and that by improving his reading skill, he can make tomorrow a better day than today.

In the following pages, we will try to help you do your job. We suggest that you read through the whole manual before you meet your student or students. After you have met your students, you should reread the manual, paying special attention to the sections that deal specifically with students like yours; mark the portions to which you will want to refer later.

Teaching can be a rewarding experience for you. Be patient. As your student learns, you too will learn.

Why Some People Have Difficulty
Learning to Read

Reading is one of the most complicated skills developed by man. To sense the impact of printed symbols on a beginning reader, try to read this:

ノーϞ ϮϮ ϟϡΝ ϟϮ϶Ν ϟーハ Ϩθθ ʃーーϽ ϣΝϟ
ϟー ϟーϽΝ ϟー ϟϡΝ ϣϮϽ ーϟ ϟϡΝ ハΝϣϢϽΝハ

In code, this says: *Now is the time for all good men to come to the aid of the reader.*

This example may help you understand how confusing a printed page looks to a beginner or to someone who is having trouble learning to read.

To learn to read, the individual should have the proper biological equipment with which to learn and an environment that encourages learning. Difficulties in learning can come from physical handicaps, poor environment, emotional problems, and ineffective teaching. This is what we mean:

1. Biological Equipment. Since reading depends so heavily on the senses of seeing and hearing, any student with a defect in either area will have special difficulty. Should you suspect that your student has a problem in vision or in hearing, inform your supervisor so that he may assist in having it corrected.

In some cases, a student may not learn because of limited intellectual capacity (sometimes called low IQ). The number of such people in the general population is small. This is true even among the group that you teach. Your basic assumption must be that every student you deal with *is able* to learn more than he has already learned and that you will help him to do so.

2. Environment. Every child from the time of birth is exposed to the many different sounds and sights of his home and neighborhood.

But the child who has been drawn into few conversations or discussions will lack the vocabulary to express his feelings or to describe many things and ideas. If, for example, no one has ever chatted with him about big and small, tomorrow and yesterday, the days of the week, or the months of the year, these concepts will be vague for him. If no one has ever read to him, or shown him pictures, or described sights outside his little world, or taken him on trips, he will be handicapped as a reader. The degree of handicap will vary from one student to another.

You are in a position to help compensate for this early lack of stimulation and experience. No matter what the age of your student, child or adult, your teaching, conversation, and reading aloud can help overcome this handicap.

Students coming from a home where a foreign language is spoken may have the necessary vocabulary and concepts—but only in their mother tongue. They sometimes fail to learn to read simply because they lack familiarity with the sounds of the English language. Conversation in English is particularly important for them.

Children coming from homes in which education has been limited in the past, in which the book is not valued, are frequently not expected to succeed at school. This may be the attitude of the parent and, in some instances, it may be the attitude of the teacher. Unfortunately, such children can easily absorb the feeling that learning is not really worth the trouble it takes.

It should be remembered that people generally rise to meet expectations: your attitude should be that you expect the student to work hard and to succeed in learning what he is supposed to learn. Your attitude will have a beneficial effect on his attitude toward learning.

3. Emotional Problems. Emotional factors are inevitably intertwined with reading difficulties. Even when they are not the primary cause of the reading difficulty, emotional problems are bound to develop in every case of reading failure. Reading failure is school failure, and because the school is generally important in present-day life, the emotional ill effects of school failure spread to other aspects of an individual's performance.

The student who fails can easily come to believe that he is stupid, that he is inadequate, and that he is worthless. His behavior reflects these feelings and serves as a further deterrent to learning. He is unable to pay attention and becomes restless and impatient. He may seek some other interest or outlet for his energies, and become disruptive in class.

Problem readers are thus all too often seen as "bad" children, and *they see themselves* as "bad" children. They are impatient, unable to wait for things they want; a desire for something is translated into immediate physical movement. Despite their apparent competence and confidence in some situations, such children suffer from a lack of self-esteem. Convinced that they are hopeless failures, they lose all confidence that they can learn. As they grow older, reading backwardness dooms them to continued failure in school. As their feelings of misery pile up, they are absent more and more, and finally they give up and drop out altogether.

Because of this chain of failures, they are deprived of the opportunity to enrich their lives through rewarding jobs and the pleasurable use of leisure time. They become dependent on others for the interpretation of the written word. In cases where the text is a contract for an installment-plan purchase or a lease, the disabled reader is an easy prey for exploitation by the dishonest.

4. Inadequate Schooling. Poor teaching can account for some cases of failure to learn to read. Also, even in this day and age, some students will come to you who have never had the opportunity to go to school. This last group cannot be called failures. They can learn quickly, once you convince them that it is not too late to start.

Since a cause is rarely simple or isolated, it is probable that a combination of the foregoing factors has contributed to the failures of the students with whom you will deal.

What You Should Know about a Reading Program

WHY STUDENTS COME TO READING PROGRAMS

Some are sent by their school teachers. Others come on their own, having their doubts, yet willing to try. They hope that you may help them break out of their pattern of failure. Some are brought by their parents. All have very specific goals, ranging from the most modest to the most challenging. Among these goals are the following:

1. To be able to keep up with studies at school.
2. To be able to read street and subway signs.

3. To gain self-respect and the respect of others.
4. To be able to read documents requiring signature, such as leases and contracts.
5. To be able to fill out an application blank for a job.
6. To be able to read a book as other people do.
7. To learn to read the Bible.
8. To be able to help their children with their school work.
9. To learn to be better parents.
10. To seek a social outlet — to have something to do and someone to talk to.
11. To be able to read newspapers and magazines.
12. To be able to read on a higher level in order to qualify for the many types of jobs in the service occupations that require a higher reading level, or for vocational upgrading.
13. To be able to acquire the high school equivalency certificate. A minimal requirement for many jobs that represent true upgrading, this certificate also admits the possibility of higher education.

To help your student master his difficulties in reading, you must keep these goals in mind, the better to motivate him to learn and to sustain his interest. With heightened interest and success, with improved study habits, he will develop the ability to reach for higher levels of achievement and to persist in working toward them. As he is successful, the student will gain an improved image of himself and a confidence in his ability to learn.

The tutor should try at all times to make reading pleasurable. Hopefully the student will learn to read well enough so that he will widen his horizons and deepen his awareness and enjoyment of life.

WHERE REMEDIAL PROGRAMS MEET

Remedial programs are sponsored by settlement houses, community centers, churches, government agencies, and other helping organizations. They may at times be conducted in rooms that are noisy, lack privacy, and were never designed for teaching. The teacher may have to suffer many unavoidable minor inconveniences because the sponsor is unable to arrange better housing.

If you are on the planning committee for a new program and have a voice in choosing a site, you should know that it is best to avoid meeting in a school; for many students, walking into a school building may have unhappy past associations that interfere with learning.

No matter where you meet, one precaution is important: be certain that older students are protected from the prying and sometimes unkind eyes of young children, who may ridicule them because they require remedial instruction, or because they are learning "baby" work.

HOW OFTEN TUTORING SHOULD TAKE PLACE

Learning is most successful when there is frequent repetition and reinforcement. For your services to be most effective, you should meet with each student at least two times each week, for an hour each time. The student will learn more if he meets the tutor for one hour twice a week than if he has one two-hour session once a week. The more frequently you meet, the more quickly the student will learn.

QUALITIES NEEDED IN THE TUTOR

Because of the "crash" nature of many programs, much of their success depends on the good judgment and ingenuity of the tutor. Remember that you are now working in a professional capacity as an auxiliary staff member. You are working with a team of professionals who will appreciate your dedication to the program. You will be expected to have:

1. Respect for your students.

2. Absolute confidence in their ability to learn.

3. Patience; this is a long haul.

4. Acceptance of the student as a person. Never scold, never reproach. Remember that you are there to help him learn to read; he has not applied to you for therapy or for "remaking" as a person.

5. Flexibility. Each thing may be taught in many ways; try to create many ways yourself, remembering to present new material in novel and interesting ways that appeal to the senses of sight, hearing, and touch. Inquire into the methods and techniques of other teachers, and borrow what is useful to you.

6. Adaptability. You must always work cheerfully with your student, despite the inconveniences of noise, lack of privacy, inadequate equipment, and insufficient and inappropriate materials. Improvise: large sheets of white paper will substitute for a blackboard; a screen will serve as a partition.

7. Knowledge of the skills to be taught, or readiness to learn those skills. Your reading of this manual, for example, indicates a readiness to learn these skills.

8. Commitment to the program of tutoring. This requires a definite commitment of time. If you are entering this program on trial, with the feeling that you may have to drop out if you do not enjoy it or for some other reason, indicate this to the director of the program. He will then take this into account in assigning you.

9. Ability to maintain an ethical, professional relationship with the student. His confidences must at all times be respected. The student must never be discussed with anyone but the teaching supervisor. Much harm can be done in casual talk or gossip.

10. Model behavior. The tutor is not expected to be perfect. He is, however, expected to serve as a model for the behavior of the student. Remember that until now your student has learned largely by observation and imitation. By virtue of the tutor's punctuality, courtesy, speech, and appropriate dress, the student learns what is expected of him; it is not necessary to discuss such things with him explicitly. If he learns to respect the tutor, he will adopt him as a model. Sometimes the gains may not be apparent until long after you have terminated instruction.

HOW THE TUTOR RELATES TO THE SUPERVISOR AND OTHER STAFF MEMBERS

The staff in your tutorial program is a team working together to help solve the problem of illiteracy. Some members of the team have more experience and training than you; some may have less. But remember, all of you are working together.

You have much to give, and much to learn; you may have questions about things you see being done, or not being done. Ask these questions of the person responsible; try to avoid jumping to conclusions; try to avoid being destructively critical and stirring up tempests. Remember that everyone involved is trying and that no one way of doing things has yet been proven to be best. Be tolerant of a certain degree of disorganization, and accept the fact that there are problems.

When you have questions about technique and problems in relation to a particular case, be sure to ask for assistance. Such requests reflect your sincere effort and interest and will earn you the respect of the staff.

HOW THE TUTOR RELATES TO THE STUDENT

1. Be sure you know your student's name, or his nickname, or both, and how to pronounce and spell them properly.

2. Be sure that he knows your name.

3. You will want to get to know your student as a person, by talking to him privately. Assure him that there is nothing to fear and that returning to "school" will be pleasant and profitable. Remember his mixed feelings about coming for instruction. He needs constant reassurance and encouragement. He must feel that he is successful, useful, and needed; that he is understood and liked in spite of his faults; and that you have confidence in him.

4. Do not overidentify with the student. Be warm, friendly, and accepting, but not too personal. Keep this a professional relationship.

5. Do not pry into his personal life and affairs. As he gets to know and trust you, he will tell you more and more about himself. Do show your interest in him as well as in those interests that should furnish working material for your instruction. There is a delicate line between real interest and prying; try to remain on the right side of that line.

Sometimes the student will relate stories of deplorable and distressing conditions within the home or at school. The tutor, though a sympathetic listener, should report these to the supervisor, when appropriate, but he must be aware that some of these reports may be fantasies created for a willing and responsive listener. The supervisor will arrange to verify the reports and confer on any further helpful action that may be appropriate. Problems relating to welfare services, clothing, and medical and psychiatric help should all be handled in this manner.

As you get to know your student, you will find that he has many, many problems. You alone cannot solve all of his problems. The area of your responsibility is clearly limited to that of reading.

6. Do not be patronizing.

7. Do not give the student money.

8. Never break an appointment without notifying the student.

9. If a student is absent, find out why. A telephone call or a home visit may help. He may be afraid to return if he is out too long. When he returns, inquire about his health; do not reproach him.

10. Arrange to have your student call the office if he must miss an appointment, or will be late. This will encourage in him a feeling of

responsibility to you and to the program. Do not be too disappointed if the student breaks an appointment, or if he fails to call.

11. If you are teaching in the neighborhood in which your students live, walk around and become familiar with it. This will help you know your student better and will also give you something more to talk about with him.

GENERAL INSTRUCTIONS TO THE TUTOR

1. Praise the student as frequently as you can, but only for genuine success. Indiscriminate praise is not helpful. The student perceives it as insincere; it defeats its purpose.

2. Explanations and directions must be clearly given, in very simple words; do not talk above the student's head; do not talk down. Assume that if the student does not understand, there is something wrong with your techniques or your explanation, not with the student.

3. There must be no suggestion of criticism of the adult or child who does not read well. Criticism may destroy self-confidence and interest in learning. Needless to say, do not ridicule the student; do not shame the student; never, never be sarcastic.

4. Many of your students will have dialects and accents, making their speech different from yours. Your primary purpose is to teach reading. Too many corrections of his speech are interpreted by the student as criticism, and will destroy his interest in learning. Do not correct speech. Limit your corrections to those that affect the meaning of words. This is a very subtle and difficult point: it is essential to correct only important errors. Accept the student's speech, keeping in mind that it is completely appropriate in his cultural group. Let him say "ain't," or retain his dialect or accent. Concentrate on helping him understand what he reads in English.

If you feel, however, that the student's speech is a serious handicap to him, then you should ask your supervisor whether a speech specialist is available to evaluate that problem. But you will not be helping him if you step into that area in addition to reading.

5. The manner in which you react to errors is very important. It is more constructive, when the student has made an error, to correct it casually, rather than to overemphasize it by asking questions to lead him to correct himself. Tell the rule, instead of asking. If it is appropriate, teach and reteach the point, but do not make an issue of the error itself.

6. Remember that it is your responsibility to plan carefully for the lesson, and at the same time to be flexible, taking your cues on content from the student. Build on your student's strengths and interests. The girl who likes to cook will learn to read recipes, though she may resist formal reading instruction.

7. Never promise anything that you cannot deliver. Be very careful not to make any commitment to the student based on something promised to you by someone else; if that person disappoints you, you will have to disappoint the student. Remember that when you break a promise, you are joining a long line of others who have broken promises to this student. You must make every effort to show him that he can have confidence in you, and that your promises are meaningful. If you promise a trip, or a party, or a gold star, keep that promise. Avoid promising anything that is not within your power to deliver − a job, a promotion, a certificate, or even a reading grade level.

8. While setting higher horizons for your student, help him maintain a realistic evaluation of his strengths and limitations. A sixteen year old boy who reads at the second grade level must continue to aspire to improve his reading, but it is not helpful to encourage him in his dreams of entering a profession that involves graduate work, such as medicine. Similarly, a boy who cannot count should not be encouraged to try to become an accountant.

9. The teacher must plan for the student to make some progress each day, and to know what success he is having. Without some planning, failures and frustration result. These are disastrous with your students.

10. Be careful not to overwhelm or overburden the student. He must leave each lesson with a real sense of enjoyment and achievement.

11. Keep an accurate attendance record. It will help you later when you try to evaluate his progress.

12. Try to give a certificate at the termination of a set number of lessons.

13. Be careful about presenting choices. If you ask, "Do you want to−?" the answer may be "No!" If you ask, "What do you want to do?" the answer may be a suggestion completely unacceptable to you, such as "Go to the movies." It is wiser, instead, to offer alternatives: "Shall we read the newspaper or the magazine today?" Be certain that each of the choices is one really available to the student. For example, he may choose to read one of two books on the shelf, both within his

reading level. Or he may choose to go on a trip with you on Saturday or Sunday (not on a school or workday, if either of you is occupied on those days), to the museum, or zoo, or airport, but not to a place for which the admission charge is prohibitive. Remember that offering the choice of many things makes it difficult and confusing for the student to make a decision.

14. Avoid asking questions to which the student need give only one-word answers, particularly "yes" and "no." Instead, ask questions that encourage longer answers: "Tell me about the TV show you saw yesterday," or "What are you planning to do this weekend?"

15. When playing games with your student, do not arrange to lose so that he will win. Play honestly; he will know if you lose deliberately.

16. Be patient. Progress is very slow. You cannot hope to teach overnight what your student has failed for years to learn. You cannot hope to undo overnight the damage that has occurred over a period of years.

Tips on Techniques

INTRODUCTION

You may find that the people you teach are not able to concentrate on one thing for more than a few minutes. People who are thus easily distracted are said to have a brief attention span. Because such students grow restless and lose interest quickly, you must plan to have many interesting activities ready for the hour, and to shift frequently from one activity to another. In addition, the attention of the restless student may be cut off by noise and movement. Ideally, the physical conditions under which you teach will be such that there are few distractions. Actually, you may find the physical conditions very uncomfortable; you may be in a noisy place where people pass by frequently; the light may be poor and there may not be a blackboard. You may even have to find yourself a different corner each week. Depending on the nature of the program in which you are working, you may not be able to do much about some of these conditions. Try not to compromise on the following:

- Assure older students absolute privacy from younger children

- Use the same location for each lesson

- Arrange to have enough light, particularly for the student; if necessary, bring a small table lamp for this purpose

- If you can't avoid noise, try to set up a screen or a barrier of furniture to avoid visual distractions for the student; if necessary, have the student sit facing the wall or the window so that his view will be as undisturbed as possible

SPECIFIC AIDS
About Notebooks, Files and Printing

1. Remember that beginners find it easier to read writing and printing that is large and has ample space between the lines. You should therefore use the manuscript printing that is used in the elementary grades. Here is what manuscript printing looks like.

This is manuscript printing

Manuscript printing is easier for the student to read because it is more consistent; use it in your writing for the beginner. Be sure that you print each letter clearly and consistently each time. Since the beginning reader has great difficulty in distinguishing one letter from another, ordinary handwriting may add to his confusion.

Your everyday penmanship is called cursive writing. It is usually taught in the third grade. Here it is.

This is cursive writing

2. When you teach your student new words, or words that he finds difficult, prepare an individual file of word cards for each student. Using a felt-tipped pen or heavy crayon, print one word on each card. Separate the cards into three groups: those he knows well (these

become *Friends*); those he does not know (these are *Strangers*); and those he may know at times, but with which he still needs practice (these are *Acquaintances*) If possible, obtain a metal or wood box in which each student can maintain his file. Have him file the *friends* alphabetically. Drill for a few minutes at each session, so that some of the *acquaintances* become *friends* and can be added to the file, and to enable some of the *strangers* to become *acquaintances*. The movement of each word into the *friends* file represents a real achievement for the learner.

3. Prepare two folders for each pupil: one will be a student's folder, and one a tutor's folder. Keep all of the student's work in his folder, neatly arranged. If you are working with a young child, have him make a drawing on the folder, to personalize it; encourage him to take pride in his work. At the end of the semester, you may send home samples of his work selected from the folder.

4. Have the student keep a hard-covered note book. If it is inappropriate for him to carry it home, or if he has no homework assignment, keep it in his folder between lessons. Have him work neatly in it, and take pride in its appearance. Some teachers have been very successful in having students practice on loose paper and rewrite beautifully in the hard-covered notebook, which then becomes a source of pride.

About the Lesson

1. Know what you are planning to do during each lesson. A sample plan might be:

- Present a new concept (five minutes)
- Review and drill consonant blends (five minutes)
- Discuss coming trip to museum to see Egyptian mummies (ten minutes)
- Write a story about our plans for the trip (dictated by student to teacher), read it back, learn the words, and add to the student's file of friendly words (twenty minutes)
- Read from book, continued from previous lesson (ten minutes)
- Play word game (ten minutes)

Another sample plan appears on page 83.

2. Try to teach something new at the beginning of each lesson, in order to maintain the student's interest. At the end of the lesson, it is very helpful to summarize what has been done that day. Include some

mention of each new achievement: a word, a paragraph read, something clarified.

Do not assume that your student remembers what he was taught at the last session or several sessions earlier. It is important to review the latest skills taught until you are confident that the student knows them well and is not likely to forget them. Include a five-minute review in some part of the session. Your notes on each lesson will tell you which of the skills covered last time should be reviewed today, and today's notes will remind you of what needs review at the next session.

3. Check all the written work your student does during the lesson. Do not rely on his comparing his answers with those on answer sheets provided by some publishers. Remember that a good deal of the student's learning develops as a result of the personal relationship you establish with him. When you check his work, you quickly become aware of his errors, and are in a position to clear up areas of confusion immediately. An answer sheet cannot replace you.

4. Find a book in which the student is interested, but that is above his reading level. (Remember that his interests and comprehension are beyond his reading ability.) Spend several minutes of each session reading it to him. Discuss it with him. By doing this, you are giving him pleasant associations with the printed word. At the same time, you are encouraging him to express himself, an important prerequisite for reading.

5. To further encourage a relaxed teaching atmosphere, discuss television shows with your student. Have him tell you the story of a show he watched. Discuss magazine pictures and newspaper stories with him. Assign a show of particular interest to him, and later discuss it with him.

6. At the end of each lesson make a note in the tutor's folder of what you did and your immediate thoughts on what you want to remember to do next time. Do not rely on your memory. Also note anything that the student said or did that you may want to discuss with your supervisor. In some centers, the supervisor may have a form on which you may make these notes and reports. Where no such form is provided, it is helpful to staple to the inside cover of the tutor's folder a sheet of paper on which to make your regular notations. Always remember to date your entry. When the sheet is full, do not turn it over; staple another sheet over it, with the staples at the top of the sheet, so that you can always read all the notes by picking up the top leaves.

7. Students can help students. If you should be teaching several

students at a time, you may find it helpful to have some of the students help others so that you can offer special individual assistance. When such assignments are judiciously made and carefully supervised, this procedure can work out well.

8. Sometimes you will find your student reluctant to read aloud to you, even when you are teaching him alone. It is very helpful, then, if you take turns reading aloud with him. Be cautious about criticizing even slight reading errors during the early phases of instruction. Since your goal is to encourage relaxation and a decrease in self-consciousness, such criticism may be self-defeating in its inhibiting effect on the student. Should he have difficulty with a word, supply it. If he has difficulty with too many words, the selection you are reading is too difficult. Shift to an easier selection.

9. Homework must be handled sensitively. There is no hard and fast rule about assigning homework to students in remedial programs. Assignments must be optional for the student; if they are likely to destroy his interest in the instruction, avoid homework completely. If the student asks for it, give him an assignment. Be sure to check it when he returns. He will be very disappointed if you forget, and may fail to do the work the next time. Do not reproach him if he has not done it, but assign no more until he requests it.

About Additional Aids

1. The public library is an invaluable source of material for a reading program. The librarian will help you by providing interesting books and periodicals that you might not otherwise find. After she knows your needs, she will be happy to locate appropriate materials for you, and to lend to you on special loan, for a longer-than-usual period, books that will be helpful to you. Take your student to the library if you can, when you find him willing to go. You may find that he will be very proud to own a library card of his own; help him register for one. Do not urge him to accompany you to the library if he seems to have unpleasant associations with it.

Your student may ask to borrow books from the program at times; if you can spare the books, it is worth lending them. Again, do not reproach him if a book is not returned. Ask for it once and no more; if a student fails to return a borrowed book, do not lend one to him again.

2. Tabloid newspapers, comic books, and picture magazines frequently appeal to your students. Use these materials, at the appropriate reading level, to teach critical evaluation of reading material. They can be very helpful in motivating your students to

read, to enjoy reading, and to feel success at their present levels of instruction.

3. Field trips are valuable. Plan to take your student to places he has never visited, preferably where the admission is free. Such visits should not replace regular instruction time too often. Discuss the visits in advance, and emphasize the things to look for and expect. Afterward, have the student discuss and write about the visits, or dictate stories to you about them. Concentrate on the pleasures of the visit, and the excitement of discovering one of the many wonderful things nearby. Take care to avoid making the afterwork an unpleasant burden.

Exciting places to visit include museums, zoos, theaters, concerts, the local newspaper plant, industrial plants, a fire house, park, ferry boat, historic buildings, and monuments. You will be surprised at how new all of these things will be to most of your students.

4. Encourage your student (especially the beginning reader) to read signs everywhere: road signs, street signs, signs on TV, advertising signs and labels, and signs at work and at school. Cut advertisements out of magazines. Boys will be particularly interested in automobile names and in traffic signs such as STOP and DETOUR. If your student is interested, make a file of these signs, treating them as you do his word file, that is, as *Friends, Acquaintances,* and *Strangers*.

5. Magic Slates, felt-tipped pens and magic markers, crayons, and colored pencils add variety and interest to written work.

6. To make your material go farther, and to make it easier to select exactly what you want, you will find it helpful to cut up two copies of a workbook or books of reading exercises. Staple each page to a sheet of oak tag or stiff cardboard; file the sheets in a carton or filing cabinet. Use each sheet of practice material as needed, and then replace in the file. This permits maximum utilization of a limited amount of teaching material. An additional advantage is that this practice discourages the tutor from leaning heavily on one workbook, a procedure that may prove boring to the student. Be careful not to let workbooks substitute for teaching.

If you do not have enough workbooks to cut up, use transparent material, such as tracing paper, onion skin paper, or a sheet of clear acetate, to cover the page you wish to use; have the student write his answers on the transparent material, so that the workbook remains clean. (If you use clear plastic sheets, the student can write on it with crayon that can be wiped off.)

7. An excellent means of encouraging self-expression is to dramatize different situations. Role-playing is an interesting and effective

activity for all age groups. Although it may be more exciting when done with groups of students, it can also be managed very nicely in individual instruction, with the tutor and the student acting, or role-playing, together.

The telephone is a useful prop for dramatic self-expression. Many students have never handled a telephone, or have so little experience with the instrument that they become fearful in relation to it. These students should receive assistance in learning the mechanics of making a phone call. (The local telephone company will sometimes make sample instruments available to the tutor for use in such instruction.) Others will find it easier to speak into an instrument than to address a person directly. In both cases, self-expression is encouraged through the use of the phone.

Other situations and relationships that may be dramatized are those of parent and child, teacher and student, the job interview, shopping for a particular item, and how to travel.

The use of hand puppets in role-playing with children adds variety and color to the drama. Inexpensive puppets may be purchased, or they may be made at the tutoring session by drawing on paper bags and by crayoning or inking with a felt-tipped pen on old white socks.

8. A typewriter and a tape recorder are helpful in reading instruction. They may be used to stimulate interest and to add variety to the lesson. You may have the student type stories; at other times, you may type his stories. The tape recorder may be used to record progress in oral reading or to record discussions and stories; the student learns a good deal by listening to himself.

CONCLUSION

You will have failures; you may be discouraged by lack of progress; you may feel that you have been unable to make contact with your student; you may feel discomfort with a particular student.

All of these problems arise with the best of teachers and with the most experienced. That they arise does not necessarily reflect on you; ask your supervisor for advice on how to deal with them. At times, you will want to request an evaluation of a special student by other specialists if you are working in a team setting where a counselor, a psychologist, or a psychiatrist is available.

In those cases in which you feel you have not made contact with a particular student, or feel uncomfortable with him, it is your privilege to request that he be transferred to another teacher. Other students will in turn come to you from other tutors.

Concern about failures and lack of progress is the daily lot of the good teacher; should you feel such concern, your supervisor will assist you with new materials and techniques, if that is necessary, or with reassurance, if that is all that is called for.

Working with School Children

1. Because the experience and vocabulary of children is limited, trips are very important. Take the children to a pet shop, zoo or animal farm, museum, library, fire house.

2. Make a great effort to associate reading with pleasure for them; read to them for a few minutes each day. Play-act the story with them; this will help encourage self-expression.

3. Use games as part of the instruction. In enjoying the game, children learn their reading skills at the same time. Do not feel impatient because the games take so long to play. The pleasure associated with the instructional time and the satisfaction derived from every correct move made in the game are positive gains for the child.

4. Spend time having fun with words. This gives the child practice in listening to the sounds of words, an important skill in learning to read. Make rhymes. Read nonsense poems. Play games naming things that start with the same sounds or letters, like " 'A' – my name is Alice and my husband's name is Allan; we come from Alabama and we live on Amity Street." Play Geography.

5. Avoid using the same textbook and workbook for tutoring that the child is using in his classroom at school.

6. Do not assume that the child is at the reading level expected at his age – or in his grade – or even that he is at the reading level of the reading text that he uses at school. Many children use readers in school that are in fact beyond their reading levels. You will have to evaluate the child's reading level yourself; see page 39.

7. It may be helpful, where possible, to meet with the child's classroom teacher to discuss common goals and to indicate to the teacher that the child is expending additional effort outside of school.

Before doing this, however, discuss the idea with your supervisor; in some cases, he may consider the meeting inappropriate or impractical.

8. If the child comes to you directly after school, ascertain whether your project is able to provide milk and cookies, or some other light snack for the child. Hunger will interfere with his learning.

9. To help form positive associations with the learning experience, some token rewards are useful during the early stages of remedial instruction. These may be small items costing no more than a few cents, such as a ball, a set of jacks, rubber stamps, a book or some marbles; stars, which are traditional tokens of reward, are also encouraging and helpful with some children. These should not be viewed as bribes, but rather as incentive rewards. As the instruction progresses, the need for these incentives disappears; learning will then be its own reward. On occasion children will ask for "presents" even when they have not been earned. The tutor must explain simply and clearly that the prizes are rewards and are given only when earned; when the tutor is consistent, firm, and pleasant, children will accept the rules graciously.

The cost of these rewards, as that of the snack mentioned earlier, should be borne by the program, not the tutor. Frequently, cooperative community organizations and friendly businessmen will contribute or help defray their cost when they are made aware of the need for them.

10. Many children cannot stay put with one task for very long. For this reason, it is very important to prepare many different activities for the one session; before the child wearies of one activity, it is wise to shift to another. It is helpful at times to introduce some opportunity for the child to move around: to get a drink of water, or to play Simple Simon for a few minutes before returning to a new table activity.

11. Some children who present behavior problems at school will try to "test" the tutor while they are getting to know her. They want to know just what the rules are, just what they can get away with, and what the tutor will not tolerate. They may come late, or come on time but refuse to do the work, or try to shock the tutor with their language. Such behavior is best handled without reproach, but with gentle and firm reminders of what is acceptable to the tutor and what the rules are. If the child is not ready to settle down that day, it may be helpful to suspend formal instruction for the day with a reminder that you will plan to teach him the content at the next session when he is ready to work. Review your plan for the day to be sure that the activities are varied enough to assist in capturing the child's attention and cooperation more completely next time.

Working with School Dropouts

1. Although dropouts have failed academically and may consider themselves stupid, they are frequently desperately anxious to learn some of what they missed. When they dropped out of school, they were certain that they could succeed in the outside world. They did try; they found the experience bitter. Jobs are difficult to get, and even dead-end jobs are demanding. The employer wants them on the job on time, dressed properly, and the pay may be small. The work may be boring, and sometimes seems to be menial. Most of the time dropouts are unemployed, and unhappy about this. They come to your agency for some service — possibly for a job; and someone has persuaded them to try once more to learn some "schoolwork." In a sense they are challenging your program: "No teacher was ever able to teach me before. Do you think you're any better?"

You will have to rise to this challenge. Until now, no one has given them so much individual attention; no one has set for them small goals, which are in effect promises, and then kept those promises. With gentle, firm reassurance, you can build their self-confidence and help them to learn.

2. If they are beginning readers, work slowly and patiently. Be sure to seek out or create materials of interest to adults. If you have to use material designed for children, adults will usually accept them if you explain that unfortunately this is all that is available, and that, since materials are only a tool, even these materials can be helpful. As soon as possible, bring in the adult material.

3. With this group, the caution stated earlier about privacy is essential. Never permit these young adults to be taught where younger children may observe them. Also, it may be embarrassing to your student to carry books that are obviously at a low reading level; cover his books with a college book jacket.

4. As soon as he is ready for supplementary independent reading, lend him a book to read. All of his life he may have wanted to carry a book that he could read, just as other people do.

5. If the reading grade level of your student is between the fourth and ninth grades, relate all reading instruction to vocational goals. For example, if a young man is interested in being an auto mechanic, find

manuals, instruction guides, and books about cars and mechanics to arouse and maintain his interest.

6. If the reading level is at the ninth grade or higher, set the goal of achieving the high school equivalency certificate. Call the local high school for information about the examination for this certificate. Plan your instruction in relation to the examination requirements. The certificate has prestige as well as vocational and college-entrance value. It is an important goal.

7. Avoid references to school grades and to levels of ability. Have each student compete with his own record, not with that of other students.

Working with Adults

1. The suggestions made earlier with regard to privacy for older students are especially relevant to adults.

2. Remember that adults have a wide range of experience and a relatively full vocabulary, though they may be illiterate.

3. If they have never had the opportunity to learn to read, adults have not been school failures; therefore they may not have suffered as much damage to their self-esteem as dropouts have. Their self-esteem is wanting, nevertheless, because they are aware of their great handicap in daily life and in vocational competence. They, too, fear failure; they suspect that they are "too dumb" or too old to learn anything. Adults will be responsive to instruction, provided that they are treated with the utmost courtesy and respect, with praise for every achievement, and with no reproaches. Adults can discipline themselves to stick to a job and to work hard at it, if they see results. They will do homework if they feel they are learning something useful.

4. Avoid condescension in your tone, in your language, and in the materials and subject matter you select.

Working with Non-English-Speaking Students

1. Non-English-speaking students who wish to learn to read English must be taught to speak English as well. Some of these students already read in their mother tongue. Reading English for them will at first be a matter of learning to speak the language and expanding their vocabulary. For those who have never learned to read, even in their native language, oral language instruction should precede reading instruction.

2. Many non-English-speaking students understand spoken English quite well, but are self-conscious about expressing themselves. They must be encouraged to speak, with corrections limited to major rather than trivial errors. Although your area of responsibility is reading, with this group of students you may have to expand it to include speech.

> *Because these students need very special attention, read Part IV.*

What You Need to Know About Reading

DIAGNOSTIC TEACHING AND READING INSTRUCTION

The ability to read is the sum of many skills. For example, in order to read the sentence *Tom is fat*, the reader must know:

- that English is read from left to right;
- how to sound the consonants **t, m, f**;
- how to sound the short vowels **o, a**;
- how to blend consecutive sounds in words to make a smooth-sounding word: **f a t** to sound fat;
- how to recognize **is** at sight;
- that **Tom** is a proper name;
- the meaning of the word **fat**.

In reading and understanding that sentence, the reader has applied many skills, including several that he was probably unaware of.

The poor reader, or the beginning reader, may have some of the skills just listed, but not all of them. He may not recognize the word **is**, and he may have difficulty with the short vowel **a**. He will then have great difficulty in reading the sentence. Instead of attempting to teach him every skill called for in reading these three words, the teacher will first find out which skills he already possesses. The teacher will then teach the student those skills that he needs to enable him to read the sentence.

Although the example cited here has been deliberately over-simplified, it illustrates a basic rule of effective teaching: the instructor must first find out what the student knows and what he does not know; then he must proceed to teach the student the skills that he lacks. This is called diagnostic teaching: the teaching is planned around a diagnosis of what the learner does not know and what he should then be taught. The diagnosis is made after a reading inventory is prepared for the student. The method for obtaining the inventory is explained on page 42, but we shall first discuss some of the terminology used in the inventory.

GRADE LEVELS

Grade level refers to the level of reading expected of students in a particular grade in school. For example, children in the third grade are expected to read at the third grade level. A level of 3.2 means the second month of the third grade. Usually, children in the third grade are eight years old; the exceptions are those who have been held over, or accelerated, or who entered school late for special reasons.

Grade levels in reading materials refer to relative difficulty of the material and to the school grade in which a child is expected to be able to read that material. As reading skill increases, the reader is able to read more involved material and can absorb concepts of greater complexity. The number of words in a sentence, the number of syllables in the words, and the content all contribute to the determination of grade levels of reading matter.

A student's reading grade level as ascertained by testing is not necessarily an accurate indication of his true reading ability since his score may be influenced by the way he is tested, as well as by any of several external factors. (To better understand reading levels and the skills they reflect, you might ask your supervisor for a copy of a written reading test, which you can then administer to yourself and correct.) In general, a student's reading grade level is helpful to the teacher as a rough guide, before refining the diagnosis of his reading problem. To help you appreciate the significance of a given reading level, we will describe what is generally learned in each grade.

Reading-Readiness Level (Kindergarten) — Usually Age 5

The student at this level can differentiate shapes; he knows some of the letters; he has been trained in left-to-right progression; he has become familiar with books and, ideally, has pleasant associations with them.

Pre-Primer and Primer Level (First Grade) — Usually Age 6

The first grade student learns to recognize some words at sight; he learns to associate sounds with each of the consonants and with each of the short vowels. He acquires the ability to blend the sounds of a word as they appear consecutively, starting with the first sound at the left; he learns to do this smoothly, so that the word sounds natural when spoken.

Second Grade Level — Usually Age 7

The student in the second grade learns more ways in which to analyze words. He learns the consonant blends (such as **st** and **br**).

Third Grade Level — Usually Age 8

At this level the student's reading becomes smooth and fluent. Reading is no longer a goal in itself, but also becomes a tool for the acquisition of learning in other areas: history, geography, mythology, arithmetic, and fun.

Fourth Grade to Twelfth-Grade Level — Usually Ages 9 to 17

Beginning with fourth grade and continuing through the twelfth, the emphasis in reading instruction continues to be on the acquisition of skill in attacking new words, increasing vocabulary, understanding what is read, and the improvement of study skills. At every grade level, the student's vocabulary — that is, the words he comprehends and speaks as well as those he reads — expands. At every grade level, he is also expected to derive pleasure from his reading.

DESCRIPTIVE CATEGORIES

In more general terms, readers may be placed in the following categories, which are based upon grade levels:

Completely Illiterate

Persons reading at the readiness or pre-primer level may be called illiterate. Their knowledge of reading is so inadequate that it is useless in any life situation.

Functionally Illiterate

Individuals whose reading achievement is at the fourth grade level or below are sometimes called functionally illiterate. They may read sufficiently well to be able to travel — that is, they can read signs, or simple instructions — and to read an illustrated tabloid newspaper. But their reading ability is inadequate for vocational competence in any work involving more than the simplest reading. Such people cannot read instructions for assembling or repairing equipment; they cannot read contracts that they are called upon to sign, nor can they read for pleasure. Moreover, they cannot read well enough to acquire the information that is essential for every responsible citizen. Such people may easily be limited to dead-end jobs in the lowest economic rung of the job ladder.

How to Prepare a Reading Inventory

HOW TO FIND THE READING GRADE LEVEL

Use a series of graded readers. A graded reader is a school text that has a marking indicating the grade level for which it is intended. Mark off a sample of reading material near the end of each book in the series; each sample should be 100 words long. Have your student read to you, beginning with the sample you are fairly confident he can read easily. If he misses **five words or less**, have him read to you a sample of the next (more difficult) reader. Continue in this way until he makes **six or more errors in 100 words.** The book in which he misses six or more words is too difficult for him; it marks his *Frustration Level*. The highest grade level reader in which he reads 95 or more words correctly out of 100 words is his *Instructional Level*. His *Independent Level*, at which he can read without assistance, is that in which he reads 98% of the vocabulary and understands at least three-quarters of the main ideas. Usually, the student's *Instructional Level* is one grade higher than his *Independent Level* and one grade lower than his *Frustration Level*.

Many of your students will be unable to read fluently any of the texts in the series. Although they are in the higher grades, some may be able to read only a few letters of the alphabet and one or two words. Such students will be reading at the reading-readiness level or at the pre-primer level.

HOW TO TEST COMPREHENSION

Have the student read silently a story from each book in the series. Have him answer questions about the main ideas, the vocabulary, and the details. The book in which he answers correctly three-quarters of the questions is at his instructional level. If there is a discrepancy between the instructional grade level at which the student reads, and that at which he comprehends, the reading material presented to him should be at the lower level. When he comprehends more than he reads (frequently the case with retarded readers), discussions should be at a more advanced level than that of the reading material.

FOURTH GRADE LEVEL OR HIGHER

By the time he has learned to read at the fourth grade level, a student has usually learned to sound out unknown words, and therefore does not need much help in that area. If·you discover some weakness or confusion in sounding out words, see the suggestions for dealing with this problem that appear on pages 79, 80 of this manual. Otherwise, material on how to teach the student who reads at the fourth grade level or higher can be found on pages 170-175.

Concentrate on increasing his vocabulary, and on teaching him to analyze new words by breaking them down into syllables and by learning base words, prefixes, and suffixes. He must, in addition, learn study skills, so that he may use reading more efficiently as a tool in learning other subjects.

THIRD GRADE LEVEL OR LOWER

Ascertain, by means of formal or informal testing procedures (see page 42), the answers to the following questions:

1. Does your student know his left from his right?

2. Is he confused or inconsistent in following the printed line from left to right?

3. How many of the basic sight words does he know? Which words are unfamiliar to him?

4. What skills has he acquired in sounding out unknown words?

    a. Does he know the sounds of the consonants?

    b. Does he know the short vowel sounds?

    c. Does he know the long vowel sounds?

    d. Can he blend letters sounds easily to form words (s a t to **sat**)?

    e. Can he read the consonant blends (**st, br**)?

    f. Does he know the consonant combinations (or digraphs) **ch, sh, th, wh**?

    g. Can he recognize vowel combinations, such as **oa, ai, ou**, and **ow**?

    h. Can he read vowels followed by **r (ar, er, ir, ur, or)**?

5. Is his inability to sound out words the result of his not having learned to discriminate between similar sounds when he hears them? For example, can he tell the difference between **lap** and **lack**, or **some** and **sun**? Note that students with foreign accents or dialects may have difficulty in saying the sounds as you do; this is not important. It is important that they learn to hear the differences in sounds, as an aid in word recognition. (The problem of accent or dialect in speech is discussed on pages 23, 36 and in Part IV.

6. Does he understand what he reads?

    a. Does he remember the details of what he has read?

    b. Does he understand the main idea?

    c. Does he see relationships: cause and effect, and similarities and differences?

    d. Does he understand the sequence and organization of what he has read?

    e. Is he able to draw inferences and conclusions from the reading matter?

The answers to the foregoing questions pinpoint your specific goals in teaching the student. A test that is useful for evaluating some of the items just listed, particularly those relating to phonetic skills, follows. In all such attempts at evaluation, however, keep in mind that in day-to-day planning your observations are important and relevant. In addition to the specific reading skills to be observed and evaluated, the student's problems, interests, behavior patterns, work habits, patterns of speech, evidence of stammering or stuttering, motor coordination, and general skills must be taken into account. The more the teacher understands these factors, the more effective his planning will be. In addition, the teacher's observation will be of interest to the supervisor or the specialist, if it becomes necessary to consult one.

Remember that, in order to become better acquainted with the student you should chat with him about his interests, his vocational goals, his recreation, and his school experiences. In this way, you will become more aware of and better informed about your student's problems and needs and their relation to your program.

INVENTORY OF BASIC READING SKILLS*

This inventory will assist you in evaluating your student's strengths and weaknesses in beginning reading skills:

NAME OF STUDENT_____ DATE _____

TUTOR_____

CAUTION: If your student makes five consecutive errors in any group of questions that follow, move on to the next group; when he has failed in the same way in three groups, stop testing. This test, and any other administered to students in remedial instruction, must be given with great sensitivity, and must minimize any feeling of failure, frustration, and pressure on the part of the student.

I. Does he know left from right?

Ask these questions only if your student is under 12 years of age. List the responses in the appropriate column at the right.

	Correct	Hesitant	Incorrect
Point to your right eye.			
Point to your left ear.			
Which is your right hand?			
Point to your right ear.			
Point to your left eye.			
Which is your left hand?			

*Pope Inventory of Basic Reading Skills, © 1974, Lillie Pope, Book-Lab, Inc., Brooklyn, N.Y.

II. How much sight vocabulary has he?

A measure of the number of words the student can read at sight is made by asking him to read from a list of commonly used English words. A sample will be found on page 46. Present to the student a set of cards with these words on them. Ask him to make two piles: knowns and unknowns. Have him read to you the pile of words he knows. Count those he reads correctly. His sight vocabulary is _____ words.

III. Can he hear the initial consonants? (Auditory Recognition of Initial Consonants)

Say, "I shall say a word to you. Write the sound that you hear at the beginning of the word." Samples: **(b) boy; (s) seem.**

If the student fails to write correctly ten of the sounds, ask him to repeat the sounds to you. Thus you will know whether he hears the sound correctly, even though he is not yet able to write the letters associated with the sounds.

1. **(d)** daily	8. **(j)** jam	14. **(t)** timber
2. **(g)** gown	9. **(r)** rabbit	15. **(w)** walnut
3. **(s)** sober	10. **(b)** barber	16. **(y)** yes
4. **(m)** marry	11. **(p)** pile	17. **(k) (c)** kangaroo
5. **(f)** fish	12. **(l)** lazy	18. **(z)** zero
6. **(h)** happy	13. **(n)** naughty	19. **(v)** violent
7. **(c)** cat		

IV. Can he hear the final consonants? (Auditory Recognition of Final Consonants)

Say, "I shall say a word to you. Write the sound that you hear at the end of the word." Samples: **rap (p); leg (g).**

Follow the instructions given for section III.

1. bird **(d)**	5. half **(f)**	9. sedan **(n)**
2. dialogue **(g)**	6. topaz **(z)**	10. fight **(t)**
3. miss **(s)**	7. lock **(c,k)**	11. robe **(b)**
4. stream **(m)**	8. boil **(l)**	12. soup **(p)**

V. Can he blend separate sounds to form a word?

"I will say two sounds. You tell me what word they could make. **a t.** At is correct. Let's try one more. **Th ing. Thing** is correct. Now try these."

l ip	ro b	s ell	f a n
t op	c u ff	bi n	m e t

VI. Can he recognize the consonants and associate the correct sounds with them? (Visual Recognition of Consonants)

Print the consonants on individual cards. Present each card, saying, "These letters have sounds. Can you sound them?"

When you present the letters (c) and (g), remember that each has two sounds. If the student gives one of the proper sounds, tell him that is correct, and ask if he also knows another sound for that letter.

If the student finds it difficult to sound the letters, say "Can you think of a word that starts with this sound?"

List the responses in the appropriate columns below.

Correct	Hesitant	Incorrect

VII. Can he read the short vowel sounds in words?

Print each pair of words on a card.

Present the cards to the student to read.

fed	lag	rot	lit
fad	lug	rut	lot

fin	rip	lip	gam
fen	rap	lop	gum

VIII. Can he read the short and long vowels? (Reading Knowledge of Vowels)

"Read these words as well as you can." Present each word on a separate card.

1. mat   3. let   5. bin   7. rob   9. fun
2. mate 4. mete   6. fine   8. robe   10. fume

IX. **Does he reverse?**

Present the following words on cards and say "Read these words."

1. pal	7. tops	13. won
2. no	8. meat	14. rats
3. raw	9. never	15. nap
4. tar	10. even	16. read
5. pot	11. saw	17. lap
6. keep	12. tan	18. was

X. **Can he hear the consonant combinations? (Auditory Recognition of Consonant Blends and Digraphs)**

Say, "I shall say a word to you. Write the sound that you hear at the beginning of the word. This sound will be a combination of two or more letters." Samples: **(ch)** chicken; **(sp)** speak.

Follow the instructions given for Section III.

1. **(sm)** smoke	11. **(pr)** practice	20. **(sn)** snore
2. **(dr)** drive	12. **(sl)** sloop	21. **(fr)** frank
3. **(th)** thank	13. **(str)** stripe	22. **(spl)** splendid
4. **(gr)** grow	14. **(cl, kl)** clay	23. **(sh)** shape
5. **(pl)** plaster	15. **(sk)** skill	24. **(spr)** spring
6. **(gl)** glue	16. **(fl)** flower	25. **(br)** brass
7. **(sk)** skate	17. **(cr, kr)** crank	26. **(sw)** swing
8. **(ch)** choose	18. **(wh)** wheel	27. **(bl)** black
9. **(tr)** trip	19. **(scr, skr)** scream	28. **(sp)** sparrow
10. **(st)** stand		

XI. **Can he recognize the consonant combinations? (Visual Recognition of Consonant Blends and Digraphs)**

Print the following combinations on separate cards. Present each card to the student, saying, "Can you tell me a word that starts with this sound?"

sh, ch, th, wh, sm, dr, gr, pl, gl, sk, tr, st, pr, sl, str, cl, fl, cr, scr, sn, fr, spl, spr, br, sw, bl, sp

List the responses in the appropriate column below.

Correct	Hesitant	Incorrect

XII Can he read the vowel combinations? (Reading Knowledge of Vowel Combinations including Vowels followed by "r")

Present the following words on cards, saying, "Try to say these words as well as you can, even if you have never seen them before."

1. coal	8. avoid	15. harm
2. burn	9. nook	16. meant
3. morn	10. spray	17. term
4. bawl	11. laid	18. joy
5. low	12. firm	19. howl
6. free	13. lout	20. brew
7. leak	14. maul	21. took
		22. lie

COMMON SIGHT WORDS

Some words are encountered so frequently in reading that it is helpful to learn them very quickly, even before the rules for sounding them out have been mastered. Many of these words will already be familiar to your students.

A list of commonly used English words is shown below.

the	in	one	she	about	can
of	*that	you	*there	into	only
and	is	I	would	*than	other
*was	*on	this	*their	him	new
he	be	had	we	been	some
*for	at	not	if	has	could
it	by	are	out	*when	time
with	or	but	so	who	these
as	have	*from	said	will	read
his	an	were	*what	more	may
to	*they	her	up	*no	*then
a	which	all	its	*them	do

first	should	*never	thought	city	love
any	because	day	pretty	give	full
my	each	same	*went	let	am
*now	just	another	say	big	girl
like	those	know	call	eat	walk
our	people	thank	school	*saw	draw
over	*how	us	*every	best	*run
man	too	great	don't	*ever	black
me	little	old	does	light	play
*even	please	year	get	thing	soon
*most	good	off	left	*want	try
made	very	*come	buy	done	woman
after	make	go	*always	open	exit
did	still	*came	*away	kind	today
many	own	right	funny	help	two
before	see	take	put	show	danger
*must	stop	bring	think	write	poison
through	work	house	enough	gave	keep
back	long	use	far	today	seem
*where	get	again	better	white	send
much	here	goes	why	tell	
your	between	around	find	together	
way	start	home	going	keep	
well	both	small	look	boy	
down	under	found	ask	peace	

*Note: Many of these common sight words present a particular challenge to children with reading problems. Some are easily reversible (as **on** and **no**); others differ only in subtle ways, such as having one letter in place of another (came - come). Those marked with an * are the most frequently confused. In order to learn to recognize them easily, remedial students require a great deal of practice with each of these words.

The foregoing list is from: *Sight Words for the Seventies,* © 1974 Lillie Pope, Book-Lab, Inc., Brooklyn, N.Y.

PART 2

How To Teach

Methods of Teaching Reading to Beginners

There are many methods of teaching reading; frequently you will read assertions by one group that they know how to teach reading better than does another group, or that a new method of teaching has been invented. Actually many methods can work with a large majority of students. For the most part, however, you will be trying to teach students with whom some particular method has not worked. Several of the leading methods will be described to you briefly, chiefly to acquaint you with them. (For more detailed information, consult the references in the appendix of this book.) Before describing the methods, however, we present the important distinction between developmental reading instruction and remedial reading instruction.

Developmental reading instruction is the term applied to the systematic teaching of reading skills to students *who have not been taught those skills before*; these students acquire the elementary skills, progressing from one skill to the next. Ordinarily, you will be giving developmental reading instruction only to a very small group of adults — those who are trying to learn to read for the first time and who have never been exposed to any kind of reading instruction.

Remedial reading instruction, in contrast, is meant for those students who have been exposed to instruction but have failed to learn what was expected of them. Generally, such students have learned *something,* and have learned it unevenly. Nearly all the people you will teach are in this category. With this group it is especially important to determine just what each one has learned and what he has not learned — in other words, to use *diagnostic* teaching.

Methods of teaching beginning reading may be divided into two general groups: those that teach the reader to sound out words (the decoding approach), and those that teach the beginner to recognize whole words.

1. The Sight-Word, or Look-Say Approach

This method emphasizes the learning of whole words by recognition of the appearance of the total word. Each word must be memorized independently. Languages using ideographic writing, such as Chinese, must be learned exclusively by this method. Little children who watch TV learn many of the words in the "commercials" by this method. In school, when this approach is used, the intent is to give the child early satisfaction in getting meaning from the material he reads. Picture and context clues are helpful in recognizing words taught by the sight-word method. When enough words have been learned, it becomes important for the learner to acquire phonic skills so that he may know the rules by which he may expand his reading vocabulary. It is obviously impossible, and unnecessary, to commit the whole language to memory by sight.

2. The Decoding Approach

The decoding approach emphasizes the sounding out of words. Rules are taught for sounding individual letters and combinations of letters. By applying the rules, the student is able to sound out the words. For example, if, when confronted with the word l-a-t-e, the student has already learned that the final "e" is silent, giving the "a" the long "a" sound, he can sound out this word correctly. Since English is not a completely phonetic language, there are many exceptions to the rules. Nevertheless, there is enough consistency when the rules are followed for a knowledge of phonics to be essential. The Phonics and the Linguistic Methods are both examples of the decoding approach to beginning reading instruction: both teach the learner to associate sounds with letter symbols in order to "crack the code."

Teaching the learner to decode is part of every good beginning reading program. To minimize failure, and to remediate those who have failed, it is wise to teach the skills of decoding, or sounding out, in simple orderly steps.

Each of the following methods emphasizes one or the other of these approaches. *The methods are not necessarily parallel or mutually exclusive.*

A. The Initial Teaching Alphabet, or ITA, or New Alphabet Method

This method was prepared in England and attempts to cope with the irregularity in English spelling by creating a special symbol for each of the 44 sounds in the language. The student learns to read from specially prepared material in which there is complete consistency between each symbol and the sound it is to represent. As his reading matures, he is gradually introduced to our standard 26 letter alphabet. By the time he is an advanced reader, he is able to read all printed matter easily, with no further reliance on his special alphabet.

B. The Color Method

This approach uses the regular alphabet and associates a color with every different sound in the language. At first the student learns to identify the color with the sound, then the color and the spelling with the sound. The color is removed gradually as he begins to respond mainly to the spelling.

C. The Experience, or Write-Your-Own Book, Method

This approach is used by many teachers to encourage early reading experiences. It is especially valuable in remedial instruction as a technique for developing material that is meaningful and interesting to the individual student. The student dictates to the teacher a story or a series of thoughts that has great meaning or interest for him; the teacher writes down the story. If the student is able to write it, or to type it, he does so. The story becomes the student's reader; he learns the words, he reads the story, and he expands on it in his successive lessons. This is an invaluable method for capturing the interest of someone who has been difficult to reach; the crucial aspect of this method is that of getting to know just which subject is most meaningful to the student. With a child, it may be policemen, or soldiers; with a teenager or an adult, it may be marriage, or the draft, or a special vocational interest, or his own feelings about himself.

D. Programmed Instruction

This technique is designed to permit the individual student to progress at his own rate of speed; instructional material is set up in such a manner that he knows immediately if his response to a question is wrong. If he is correct, he continues; if incorrect, he may either repeat some of the work until he knows it well, or he may be given the opportunity for more drill without repeating what he has already done. This method is helpful in individualizing instruction. The programs now offered need greater refinement. In using this technique in remedial work in reading, it is well to remember that the personal contact between the tutor and the learner is invaluable; special effort must be made to retain this personal relationship when using programmed materials.

E. The Individualized Approach

Recognizing that individuals differ in their skills, their aptitudes, and their interests, many educators in the field of remedial reading attempt to suit the instruction to the individual; they use the method they deem most suitable for each learner, and frequently a combination of all the methods. Some people have superior visual memories, and learn best by seeing. Some have good auditory memories and learn best by hearing and remembering what they hear. Some learn best by using their muscles; they learn best by forming letters with their hands. With some, touch is very helpful; tracing letters with the finger on materials of different textures (sand, velvet, ice) is effective. Some need a combination of these experiences.

To be most effective, the reading teacher should use multisensory appeals: phonics for learning by sounds, sight words for learning by vision, written practice for learning by action, and cut-out letters for the additional use of the sense of touch.

Using a combination of approaches insures reaching each student in the learning style best suited for him. It also produces enough variety in the instruction to avoid monotony and to arouse and maintain the student's interest.

WHICH METHOD SHOULD YOU USE?

A. If your supervisor or your agency uses one method and directs you to use that one, that is what you should do.

B. If your supervisor does not recommend a particular method, or if there is no supervisor available, study the materials provided for you in the program. These materials will often determine the method you use.

C. If no specific method is prescribed, use the individualized approach following the guidelines set forth here, and making use of references and materials described here. Use your ingenuity, selecting materials on the basis of the interest, attitudes, and ability of the student. Following the student's interests and leads will enrich your instruction. Generally, the emphasis here will be on informal materials that are inexpensive and easily obtained, or on materials created by the teacher.

GENERAL GUIDELINES

After you have some notion of what your student knows and what he must learn, set simple goals for him, so that he may quickly achieve some success, no matter how small. You should also have some idea of your student's interests. Try to avoid reteaching him what he already knows; use what he knows to help him learn something new. Remember that every lesson must have variety and must be directly related to the interests and needs of the student. Remember that he must feel success, and you also must experience success. Remind him of the new things he has learned, but do not exaggerate.

In Part III (on page 86) you will find a very detailed list of the skills to be taught at every grade level. It may be helpful for you to study it now and to refer to it again as you need it.

Third Grade Level or Lower

If your student reads at third grade level or lower
- he may not yet have acquired the habit of looking at the printed line from left to right
- he does not yet recognize enough words at sight
- he lacks skill in sounding out unfamiliar words
- he lacks skill in breaking down long words into smaller familiar units
- his vocabulary may need enlargement
- he may be fearful of and disinterested in learning to read

Your goals, then, are to

- teach him to read automatically from left to right
- teach him a basic vocabulary that he may recognize at sight
- teach him how to sound out unfamiliar words
- teach him to analyze the structure of words as an aid in reading
- help increase his vocabulary
- help increase his comprehension of reading matter
- build and maintain his interest in acquiring reading skills

This section contains specific instructions on how to achieve these goals. Read the whole section; then select and use those elements which best meet the needs of your student.

The first step in teaching a student who has not yet mastered the elements of reading is to give him some vocabulary that he recognizes at sight. Your student will already know some words that he has learned at school or recognizes from TV advertising and daily living. You will help him increase the number of such words. These words will make it possible for him to read meaningful material while he is acquiring his sounding-out skills.

At the very same time he must be given a systematic method of approaching unfamiliar words. He should be taught the sounds of the consistent consonants, the short vowels, the remaining consonants, the long vowels, and then the remaining special sounds. He must then learn to break down long words into their component parts as an aid to reading them more easily.

As soon as he has learned to sound out the vowels, the student must be given the opportunity to read aloud to the teacher. This will give him the satisfaction of displaying his achievement to himself and the teacher. When the purpose of the lesson is to have the student sound out a word for which he has learned the rules, it is important not to read the word for him, but rather to help him figure it out. It is equally important to be tolerant of the student's dialect or foreign accent when he is sounding out. Be careful to criticize or correct only when it is obvious that the student has misinterpreted the meaning of the word. Do not correct accent or dialect if the student is reading the word as he would ordinarily say it in his own home.

Non-phonetic words (words that do not follow the rules you have taught the student) should be treated as sight words; pronounce them for the student; do not let him try to figure them out. Tell him they are exceptions to the rule.

From the very beginning of phonic instruction, it is desirable to include a great deal of spelling activity in the teaching. As the student learns to unlock words by sounding them out, he learns at the same time to apply the same skills to spelling.

If your student does not always know which is right and which is left, or if he does not always read from left to right, spend a few minutes at every session working on this problem, using the activities suggested in Part III, page 79.

STEP 1. RECOGNIZING WORDS AT SIGHT

Sight words may be taught by means of the *experience approach* as well as through the use of *word lists*. To help the student build a stock of words that he recognizes at sight, the vocabulary must be coordinated around his interests. It cannot be emphasized too often that in order for the instruction to be effective, the interest of the student must be captured and maintained continuously. If the student is applying for a job as a clerk, concentrate on words in job applications and on words used in office positions. If the family is planning a wedding, or expecting a baby, the words may be related to those subjects. Do the same if he wants to be a fireman, or an actor, or a truckdriver, or if he loves food.

The experience approach is helpful with the remedial reader in instruction at every level. Its main technique is the Write-Your-Own-Book, which is essentially a book created by the student for his own reading instruction; the teacher assists in writing down the material.

When no appropriate printed material is available for children and adults in disadvantaged areas, such homemade texts provide a successful substitute. Because the Write-Your-Own-Book is based on the interests and experiences of the individual student, it is particularly meaningful, and thus provides the best motivation for him that is available to the teacher.

How to Prepare a Write-Your-Own Book

1. First, encourage the student to talk about an interesting or dramatic experience. You may then suggest that the student dictate the story of what happened. The story may be about an interview for a job, or a ball game, or it may be a discussion of automobiles. It may even be about an incident with the landlord or police.

2. Use a felt-tipped pen for the manuscript printing. Typography should be clear, bold and black. Each page should look attractive and neat. If possible, make a carbon copy of the story at the same time. Reserve the copy for later use.

3. Use the student's natural and colloquial expressions. Do not edit or rewrite excessively. Many students tend to dictate run-on sentences or endless numbers of "and" — connected sentences. Here your guidance is valuable: keep the sentences short. Try to vary the sentence structure. Substitute periods for the "ands" without disturbing the flow of dictation. Provide for repetition of words.

NOTE: When the student dictates a contraction (can't, don't), write the word as he dictates it. After he has reread the story, it will be helpful to point out to him that this is the short form of two words that ordinarily look a little bit different: When written out, "can't" is "cannot," "don't" is "do not."

4. Clip the story into a folder; this becomes the cover for the book. Have the student print a title and his name on the cover. Encourage him to illustrate the cover and the stories, if he is a school child, or if you feel he has an interest in illustration. When practicable, photographs of the student can be used to heighten the impact of the book.

5. Have the student read the story back to you. In the course of reading the story he has just dictated, he will be hesitant about some of the unfamiliar words. Tell him those words, and then print each such word on a card. Let the student practice reading the unfamiliar words from the cards as well as the book.

6. Depending on the kind of practice that the student needs, cut the carbon copy of his story into words, or phrases, or sentences. Let him read the "cut-ups"; let him re-arrange them in new sequences, and read them back in the new order.

7. At the next lesson, review the words with him. Have him reread the story. Discuss it with him. Then, encourage him to dictate a new chapter, for which you follow the procedure just outlined.

Your student's Write-Your-Own-Book may be varied in ways that will make his lessons more interesting. It can be:

- a scrapbook, illustrated with pictures that he draws or cuts out of magazines;

- a book or play that he and you write as part of your dramatic play together;

- a newsletter or newspaper for the tutoring center.

- a "how-to" book about something he likes to do, such as "How to Build a Wooden Scooter. or "How to Build a Soapbox Wagon," or a cookbook. When making this book, it is perfectly reasonable to perform the activity at the same time, if the tutoring facilities allow for such work as baking or building. Research for the book may involve looking at library manuals, following their instructions, making shopping lists for the necessary materials and equipment, and actually shopping.

Dramatic results are possible with this technique, particularly when a teacher uncovers a subject of great interest to the student. At such times, the student may even learn to read long and difficult words (**elephant, brontosaurus**) before he learns the short, commonly used words, such as **this, then, these**.

The experience method is usually coordinated with, or supplementary to, other methods described in Steps 2 and 3.

Word Lists

In addition to the words derived from the Write-Your-Own Book, it is essential to teach as sight words the common words that make up at least 50% of all reading matter. These words are listed on pages 46-48. At each session, a few minutes should be spent learning those words that are still unfamiliar to the student. To provide variety in drilling on these and any other words or sounds the student is learning, several helpful devices are described on pages 159-165.

Any device or game that will provide interest and variety in drill should be used. Always try to appeal to as many of the senses as possible at every point: pronounce the word; have the student write it, or trace it, or feel its shape after it is cut out of materials of different textures, such as sandpaper or velvet; have the student say it or act it out.

Encourage the beginner to look for words and letters everywhere: to hunt around on the back of tin cans and cereal cartons to find letters and words that he recognizes and knows; to look at street signs and posters for numbers that he knows, for the letters in his name, and for words that he can recognize or sound out as he learns phonic skills; and to look at television commercials, magazines, newspapers, and even skywriting, with the same interest and eagerness. Every new recognition should bring with it a feeling of victory.

Abbreviations

Abbreviations are encountered frequently and may be difficult for the student to decipher. They should be taught to him as sight words. Here are some of the more common abbreviations.

| P.S. | Public School | p. | page |
| I.S. | Intermediate School | pp. | pages |

J.H.S.	Junior High School	mph	miles per hour
&	and	etc.	et cetera (and so forth)
Ave.	avenue	c/o	care of
St.	street	A.M.	morning
Blvd.	boulevard	P.M.	afternoon
Mr.	mister	P.S.	postscript
Mrs.	mistress	S.O.S.	cry for help
Ms.	miss or mistress	M.D.	doctor of medicine
Dr.	doctor	lb.	pound
D.D.S.	doctor of dental surgery	vs.	versus
oz.	ounce	C.O.D.	cash on delivery

In addition, teach the months of the year and the states of the union.

STEP 2. SOUNDING OUT UNFAMILIAR WORDS

Remember that your student already knows some of the letter sounds. Keep a list of those he knows, but do not reteach them. *In Part III you will find Sound-Out Sheets that contain word lists to assist you.*

The sounds may be taught in the following order: (1) the consonants that usually sound the same; (2) the short vowels; (3) the remaining single consonants; (4) the long vowels; (5) the remaining special sounds. For each sound that you teach, the student should learn a key word (see Part III, pages 93, 130, 131).

The Consonants That Always Sound the Same

b, d, f, h, j, k, l, m, n, p, r, s, t, v, w, z

How to Teach a New Sound

a. To teach a new sound, be sure that your student can hear the sound you are teaching, and can distinguish it from other sounds. Before you teach the letter **b**, have your student listen to the sound of **b** words: **bill, but, boy.** Then have him select the words that do not begin with the same sound from among these: **ball, bat, bounce, cat, bay.** Have him tell you words that start with the sound of **b.**

b. Now he is ready to associate the sound with its letter and with its key word (in this case, **ball**). Write a list of words beginning with **b.** Pronounce each word as you write it. Have him pronounce it, too. Have the student point out in what way the words sound the same and look the same: they all start with the same sound, and the letter that represents that sound at the beginning of each word is **b**. Once more, have him tell you other words that begin with this sound, and list them. Have him write the letter, together with the key word and its illustration, in his notebook.

Avoid giving the sound of any consonant in isolation. If the student learns the sound of the letter **b** as **buh,** it will be difficult for him to blend sounds. It is best to demonstrate the sound of **b** by saying the key word for that sound, **ball.**

c. Involve all of the student's senses in associating the letter with its sound. Have him write it in the air, on the board, on paper, in sand, with clay, or shape it with pipecleaners, while at the same time saying words that begin with that sound.

d. Now the student is ready to sound out words using the new sound. It is important to use the sound in words as quickly as possible. Present the new letter in words of one syllable, associating it with sounds that he already knows, so that he may blend them together to form a word that he can recognize: **bat.**

e. As soon as he has learned to read his new sound in words, the student is ready to practice reading that sound in sentences. Prepare sentences that use that sound frequently: **Bob** is at the **bat but Bill begs Ben** to **be** a **bit better.**

It is important to keep in mind that some students have difficulty learning new sounds; they need a great deal of practice and repetition; and their tutors need a great deal of patience.

The Short Vowels

After several of the consistent consonants with their key words have been taught, the student is ready to learn the short vowels.

Start by teaching the short **a** sound, together with its key word, **apple.** The student is then shown how this sound, placed between the sounds of two of the consonants he knows, makes a word: he can now sound out the words f–a–t and b–a–n. It is important to help him blend the sounds smoothly, to hold one sound until the next one is begun, and for him to feel satisfaction at the recognition of a word that he can now read for the first time.

He should practice blending, using his known consonants and the short **a,** as in:

tap   sad   man   dab   pan

● *Additional word lists are on page 96.*

After the a, introduce the short i sound. It can be taught in the same way, using

pin   sip   mid   fit   hip

Review the a and the i sounds by presenting a list of mixed words:

man him lit fan pin nip ran sad bit had

Teach the sound of short u.

jut   bun   rub   mud   pup

Review the three short vowels together.

jut   lip   rat   ran   sat   bun   mud   fun   sip

Following this, teach the short e. Many children find it difficult to differentiate between the short i and the short e sounds.

net   fed   hen   set   leg

Review the four short vowels.

man   pen   lit   pin   ran   net   jut   him   sad

Teach the sound of the short o:

hop   dot   bob   not   rot

Review all the short vowel sounds.

kit   not   set   ran   sun   pat
rob   hen   tin   bun   man   sot   mill

The Remaining Single Consonant Sounds

The student is now ready to learn the remaining consonant sounds, with their key words, and to use them in blending with the vowels.

c as in **cat**	c as in **cent**
g as in **gallon**	g as in **gin**

The sound of **y** as in yet and of **q** and **x** may be taught during the course of instruction when the need arises.

The Long Vowel Sounds

Because the sounds of the long vowels are the same as the names of the vowels, the student will have little difficulty learning the sounds. He must, however, learn the following instances of when to use the long vowel sounds.

1. The **e** at the end of a word is always silent, giving the preceding vowel the long sound.

fine   rave   pure   lone   sake

2. In words where one vowel follows another, the first vowel sound is pronounced by name and the second vowel is silent, as in the following double vowel words.

deem   meat   rain   oak   need

Other Special Sounds

Consonant Combinations. Teach common consonant combinations:

sl, pr, cr, fr, br, tw, pl, cl, bl, fl, gl, sc, sk, sm, sn,

sw, gr, tr, dr, sp, st, spl, spr, str, nk, ng, nt, nd

Lists of words using these combinations are on pages 106-113.

Additional Consonant Sounds. The student must learn the additional consonant sounds formed by **sh, ch, th,** and **wh.** Even though each of these is a pair of letters, the pair represents one sound, and is treated as one sound. The consonant sounds of **ph** and **ng** and **gh,** that do not occur as frequently, may be taught as the need arises during reading instruction.

sh	shop	fish	shell	shape	cash
ch	chin	chip	chop	chat	chill
th	thing	thick	thin	think	thank
wh	whiff	which	when	wheel	while

Review the special consonant sounds.

shape	play	chip	clock	thing	skin	spot
blow	flame	whip	glass	grow	pray	stiff

Additional Vowel Sounds. As the need arises, special vowel sounds should be taught to the student. At that time, systematic drill in these sounds should be given. (See word lists in Part III.)

oo as in soon	**ow** as in slow
oo as in book	**au** as in maul
oi as in oil	**ay** as in day
ow as in owl	**y** as in my
ar as in bar	**or** as in for
ir as in fir	**er** as in her
ur as in burn	

STEP 3. ANALYZING THE PARTS OF WORDS

By learning how to break down words into their parts, your student is also learning to build new words into his reading and speaking vocabulary. This should be taught directly after sound blending has been mastered. Remember that your student may already have learned some of the skills that follow.

Compound Words

Sometimes a student who can read single words is confused when these words are put together to form compound words; for him the compound word is a new word pattern. He must be helped to see compound words as two words put together. Have him practice reading the parts, and then the whole words:

news	paper	newspaper
can	not	cannot
farm	house	farmhouse
cow	boy	cowboy
grand	child	grandchild

Base, or Root Words, and Common Word Endings

To help identify base, or root, words, list a number of sets of words that have common roots. Have the student find the base word of each of the following.

asked	asking	asks	
rained	raining	rainy	
helps	helping	helpful	helper
farmed	farming	farmer	farms
running	runs	runner	
sleeping	sleeps	sleepy	

Make up exercises in which the student fills in the appropriate base word and ending. Use the base word (sing).

John is a good ____ .
Jane ____ well.
Tom is ____ a hymn.

Some endings are met frequently: s, -ed, -ing, er, est, -y, -ly. Here are sample words for practice. (Note: the student is to add the appropriate endings to each base word.)

	ask	call	help	taste	shake	slow	clean
s							
ed							
ing							
er							
est							
y							
ly							

Prefixes

Prefixes must be recognized as units, separated visually from the rest of the word. It is important for the reader to learn the meaning of the prefix, so that he may know how it alters the meaning of the base word.

The most frequently encountered prefixes are re-, in-, con-, de-, dis-, com-, un-, ex-, pro-, pre-, and en-. Note how the prefixes placed before the words in each of the following columns change the meaning of the words.

re	dis	un
fill	like	even
tell	appear	true
read	approve	fit
write	courage	lucky
print	agree	happy

Suffixes

Suffixes should be taught in the same manner as prefixes. The common suffixes are **-ly, -er, -est, -tion, -ness, -ful, -any, -ous, -ious, -ent,** and **-ment**. Note how the suffixes placed after the words in each of the following columns create new words:

ful	ly	ment	less
wonder	quick	enjoy	sleep
care	sweet	settle	pain
help	kind	improve	thought
thought	slow	agree	help

Dividing Words into Syllables

Your pupil need not know all the rules of syllabication, but he should have some understanding of how to reduce a long word to its simple elements and so read it more easily.

He must first know that every syllable must have one vowel sound, and that each vowel sound identifies one syllable. He may therefore listen to a word, count the number of vowel sounds, and thus know the number of syllables. Since only vowel sounds count, silent vowels are to be ignored. Double vowels (**oo, ee**) have one vowel sound, as do special vowel combinations, such as **ou, ow, oi, oy, ay, au, aw**.

The teacher may recite unfamiliar long words to the student, and have the student count the syllables. After the student has learned to count the syllables in a word, he is ready to divide words into syllables. He is now ready for these simple rules.

1. When two consonants are between two vowels, the syllables are divided between the consonants.

af ter   les son   bas ket   num ber

2. When a word has a vowel-consonant-vowel sequence, the consonant is usually part of the first syllable if the first vowel is short (see column A). It is part of the second syllable if the first vowel is long (see column B).

A	B
pris on	e vil
tax i	mu sic
	si lent

3. When **le** is at the end of a word of more than one syllable, the last consonant joins the **le** to make the last syllable:

ta ble	trem ble	stum ble
bu gle	rat tle	puz zle

STEP 4. DEVELOPING COMPREHENSION SKILLS

The reader must understand what he reads in order to enjoy it and use it academically, vocationally, and in everyday life. Teaching comprehension skills is therefore a vital part of reading instruction at every level.

Even in the early stages of instruction, the student understands a great deal more than he is able to read. His speaking vocabulary, his concepts, and his experience are often ahead of his ability to decipher the written symbol. After he has mastered the mechanics of reading, the emphasis in instruction should shift to increasing his understanding. From this point on, increasing his reading level means increasing his vocabulary and his ability to read and interpret more and more difficult material.

The students you teach, because of their histories of school failure and their resistance to formal learning, are all too ready to give up. The reading matter they use must be meaningful, absorbing, and useful to engage and hold their interest and attention. If it fails to involve them, they will drop instruction as soon as they have mastered the minimal skills necessary for their immediate specific goals, such as reading the subway signs, passing the driver's test, or filling out a job application. This means that the tutor must select materials for each student according to his needs, interests, and level of competence.

No matter what his age, your student has by this time acquired enough experience and vocabulary to understand a great deal about the world. Although he is unable to read the words he knows, he is able to expand his listening and speaking vocabulary.

A list of comprehension and study skills to be taught to all students is on pages 87, 88. Suggestions on how you may teach these skills at and below the fourth grade level follow.

Activities

Comprehension, as well as vocabulary, is sharpened through the use of oral discussion. Aim at clarity of thought and observation on the part of the student as you conduct the first three activities. (CAUTION: Do not assign written reports or compositions to students at this reading level. Such assignments are too difficult and will spoil for the students what should be an enjoyable and rewarding experience. Nevertheless, written work and pride in composition should be developed at this time through the Write-Your-Own book, as explained earlier on page 57). Useful activities include:

1. Discussions centering on current matters of interest to the student (housing, election issues, medical care, civil rights, play, toys, job-seeking and job-related problems, hobbies, personal interests).

2. Discussions relating to mass media that reach the student (a radio program he heard or that the tutor recommended to him, a TV program, a picture magazine article, a movie).

3. Discussions relating to visits, made with or without the tutor, in which the student discovers new things, or sees new aspects of old things, such as museums, factories, zoos, and parks.

4. Reading to the student by the teacher using material of interest to him.

5. Making lists of words in interesting categories to increase vocabulary. For example, compile a list of words for preparing meals (**food, sugar, meat, stove, oven, temperature**), for repairing automobiles (**car, engine, carburetor, mile, mileage**), or for the soldier (**draft, induction, soldier, marine**).

6. Using the student's own slang or colloquial language to help increase his vocabulary. Make a dictionary translating his words into those in more common usage; do not discourage him from continuing to use his colloquial expression, but instead assist in expanding his vocabulary based on these special words. Thus, **cool, hep,** and **jive** can be translated. These words the student uses may be unfamiliar to you. He will translate them for you. You will find your own vocabulary expanding.

Following are specific comprehension skills that the student should aim at developing, with suggested activities. Particular attention should be given to the techniques that improve clarity of thinking.

A. **Selecting the main idea:**
    Make up a title for a story, discussion, TV, or radio program.
    Select the best of several titles.
    Tell (or write at the student's level) a summary of the story or discussion.
    Select the most important sentence or paragraph.

B. **Organization of ideas:**
    Tell what happened in chronological order.
    Tell what happened in logical order.
    Organize simple sentences in the correct order.
    Organize simple paragraphs in the correct order.
    Find the answers to the questions **who, what, when, where, why** and **how.**

C. **Finding details:**

Find the answers to specific questions.

Fill in details that have been omitted in a report or discussion of a book, program, or trip.

D. **Reading directions:**

Have the student follow your directions. These should be very simple at first and become more complicated as time goes on.

Directions may involve how to find a book in the room, or another room in the building, or how to travel to a special place, or how to follow a simple construction job, a simple drawing.

Have the student give you directions for any simple project like one of the foregoing. Be sure they are complete and can be followed; if unclear, have him fill in the missing details.

In all cases, these directions should flow from the classroom work, the interests of the teacher and of the student.

E. **Drawing inferences:**

Complete a story.

Anticipate what will happen next in a story, or in current events.

Draw conclusions from information given.

Interpret the meaning of a sentence or a paragraph.

Materials

In addition to the commercial reading materials listed in Part IV, the following sources are helpful:

- Daily newspapers
- *News for You,* Syracuse University Press, Syracuse, New York. This is a high interest-level, low reading-level weekly newspaper published in Spanish and English editions for use with adult beginning readers.
- Write-Your-Own Book dictated by student
- News telecasts and radio news broadcasts
- Picture, sports and hobby magazines, such as *Ebony, Popular Mechanics, Sports Illustrated*
- Vocational material simplified by teacher
- Catalogues: mail order, sports, etc.
- Technical manuals
- Cook books

Fourth to Eighth Grade Levels

If your student reads at fourth to eighth grade levels

- he may still have some weakness in sounding out words
- he may make some of the common reading errors
- his vocabulary requires expansion
- he needs help in reading for understanding
- he needs help in learning how to study

Your goals, then, are to

help correct his weaknesses in sounding out words

help break down the patterns that cause him to make common errors

help increase his vocabulary

teach comprehension and study skills

Remember that the student's interest level is higher than his reading level. Until he is able to read easily the material that is satisfying and useful to him, it is your responsibility to motivate him to remain with the program. It is your job to retain his interest despite the difficulty in locating appropriate materials. If you can assure him (truthfully) that he is making progress, he may be satisfied with material that is not particularly interesting to him.

Look through any material you select before giving it to your student. You may find the subject matter inappropriate, and in some cases, offensive; if so, discard it. (For example, one of the adult basic readers speaks disparagingly of work done by a porter. It is obviously destructive to present such reading matter to a student who is presently occupied in such work, or to a young person whose father may be so occupied.) Try to avoid graded readers designed for young children. Also avoid reading matter that is frustratingly difficult.

If your student is fourteen years of age or older, select vocationally-oriented material. If you know your student, you will know what to look for.

You will be working on the same skills as those listed for the beginning reader, but at a higher level. At this level the student should read the material himself, when possible. Your lessons should include drill designed to correct any errors that your student makes (see page 79-80).

1. Vocabulary can be expanded at this level by teaching the use of the dictionary. Activities should include alphabetizing, finding several definitions for the same word, and analyzing the meanings of words in which the prefixes are varied, the roots are changed, or the suffixes are changed. In addition, continue to emphasize comprehension in listening, in reading, and in discussing, and begin to teach study skills.

2. Comprehension skills will be developed further by the activities described for the beginning reader in the previous section. At the present level, clarity of thought should also be emphasized, using the following techniques:

- Make an outline of paragraphs, stories, programs, and discussions
- Fill in simple outlines
- Find the author's point of view
- Select the words and phrases that are editorial rather than reportage in news items
- Differentiate between subjective and objective statements
- Seek evidence for information, when appropriate
- Identify emotionally loaded words and phrases
- Read several accounts of the same event or subject and compare them

3. Study skills may be developed through teaching the following:
- How to use the title page, table of contents, index
- How to use the dictionary
- How to use the library
- How to take notes on books and on class discussion
- How to make an outline

Materials suggested for use with beginners (page 69) and those listed in the Helpful Publications section (pages 167-178) should be used.

Ninth Grade Level or Better

Students who read at the ninth-grade level and have returned for remedial instruction are probably aware that, in order to qualify for technical occupations, a high school diploma or its equivalent (the high school equivalency certificate) is necessary. Instruction for this group involves no new skills, but rather the further development of the skills taught earlier, such as increased vocabulary, heightened understanding of material read, greater critical evaluation, better study skills, and greater appreciation and enjoyment of the printed word.

1. Vocabulary is increased by helping establish the habit of looking up words in the dictionary and by increased concentration on technical vocabulary. Keep vocabulary lists in a book or card file.

2. Comprehension skills at this level may now be developed by making much use of writing, in addition to reading.

Organization of ideas

Use all suggestions listed earlier, plus those in the following list:

- Outline a story and then write the story from the outline.
- Write an account of an event.
- Write about personal reactions to situations such as job seeking and taking a test.

Critical reading

- Look for use of propaganda devices: bandwagon, "loading the dice," glad words, bad words, glittering generalities, "plain folks."

3. Study Skills can be advanced through all the activities listed for the earlier levels, as well as by encouraging the use of almanacs, atlases, and encyclopedias. Students may be led to use these reference works by having them pursue and report on interesting research projects, such as occupational surveys, the salaries of typists, or the number of bricklayers employed in successive decades.

Materials

At this level, a great deal of reading matter is available. Encourage reading of all types of material. Allow ample time for discussion. Do not discourage the reading of pulp magazines or tabloid newspapers at this point: any reading that is successful and enjoyable helps develop reading power. As a result of your discussions and the reading matter that you can locate at the library, the reading taste of your student will be improved, and he will learn to appreciate fine literature. Remember to use

- Daily newspapers
- Magazines: picture magazines, digests, women's magazines, special-interest magazines
- Paperback book clubs: Scholastic Press (very inexpensive editions)
- *High School Equivalency Diploma Tests,* Arco Publishing Co., New York. This book is excellent for the development of comprehension and study skills; it is most useful for those interested in taking the examination to be discussed next. The book also provides opportunity for practice in taking tests, essential for your student at this point.

High School Equivalency Examination

High school equivalency programs were launched in most states after World War II to enable veterans to earn high school diplomas. The programs have been extended to include civilian adults who, having failed to complete their educations, may desire formal accreditation of their training. The high school equivalency diploma is the legal equivalent of a high school diploma for purposes of civil service requirements. It is normally accepted by business concerns and the Armed Forces as the equivalent of the high school diploma. Some colleges will accept the certificate for admission; inquiries should be made directly to the college of choice.

Information on how to file for high school equivalency tests is available from all local high schools, and from the state education departments. Although examinations are given frequently, there is a waiting list in some states. It is therefore advisable to file early, and then to embark on a course of study for the examination.

All of your students reading at or above the ninth-grade level should be encouraged to prepare for this examination. It is a realistic goal for them, and one well worth achieving.

SCOPE OF EXAMINATION

The high school equivalency examination consists of a series of five tests. They are not primarily tests of memory or of knowledge of specific subject matter. They do not call for writing on the part of the candidate. The candidate is required to select the best answer out of several choices that are given him. Each test takes approximately two hours. A brief description of each examination follows:

Test 1. Correctness and Effectiveness of Expression. Emphasis in this test is on spelling, punctuation, capitalization, and grammar.

Test 2. Interpretation of Reading Materials in the Social Studies. This test measures ability to understand and evaluate reading selections concerning social, political, economic, and cultural problems.

Test 3. Interpretation of Reading Materials in the Natural Sciences. This test emphasizes the ability to pay close attention to detail and to reason logically.

Test 4. Interpretation of Reading Materials in Literature. This test is based on a variety of selections from world literature and emphasizes the ability to interpret figures of speech, to cope with unusual sentence structure and meanings, and to recognize mood and purpose.

Test 5. General Mathematical Ability. This is a test of problem solving of a practical nature, including such things as the mathematical aspects of life insurance, installment buying, taxes, and the ability to estimate costs of simple home construction and repair projects, as well as ordinary arithmetical skills (addition, subtraction, division, multiplication) with whole numbers, percents, fractions, and decimals.

GRADING THE EXAMINATION

The mark given a candidate is determined by comparing his results with those attained by a very large group of high school seniors. *Consequently, candidates should not be discouraged by the difficulties of any of the examination items.* It is important to know that over 60% of the candidates pass the examination. This percentage demonstrates the ability of many self-educated adults to receive a satisfactory score.

Writing and Spelling

Spelling, writing, and speaking are skills that develop as reading instruction proceeds. At first, compositions are dictated to the teacher. This is done because the task of writing is difficult for the student. If asked to write, he would be unable to express the ideas that he is able to dictate. But, as his reading skill improves, so will his ability to write. At that time, he should be encouraged to write brief paragraphs that he will later develop into longer compositions. Let him write about the things he likes: describe a person he likes or dislikes; write a story about his wishes or about his best friend; describe a job; tell about an interview or the neighborhood candy store; write a song; tell what he would do if he were a landlord, or the principal of a school; write about anything of interest to him or to you.

To encourage self-expression, you must use the utmost tact and be protective of the feelings of the student. Some errors should be overlooked, if you wish to encourage expression. Concentrate on vocabulary usage and improved organization of ideas. Overlook spelling errors; they may be relatively unimportant at this time. It is not necessary that you criticize every weakness in every piece of writing. It is far better to say, "We will work on spelling at some other time," to indicate to the student that, although the spelling is incorrect, the composition has merit. Remember that encouragement and sincere commendation for improvement and for work well done are the most effective incentives for continued progress.

Arithmetic

Although your major efforts are directed at improving the communication skills of your student, he may consult you about his arithmetic. He may feel the need for some help with his homework, or he may have a serious problem in arithmetic. It is sometimes advantageous to devote part of the lesson to arithmetic work.

PART 3

Additional Aids

What to Do about Common
Reading Errors and Difficulties

*If your student is confused as to the side of the page on which to start reading, he needs practice in building the habit of reading from left to right. Check to see if the student consistently knows the difference between his left and right side. If he is hesitant or unsure, he must first be taught this. Putting a watch (a toy watch will do) on his right hand will help. Play "Simon Says" with him, making the instructions very simple: Touch your right eye, your left ear, etc. If he makes errors, demonstrate the correct response as you give the instructions. Stand or sit beside him, not facing him, when you demonstrate to him; in this way, your left hand will be at his left. If you face him, he may become more confused.

After he has learned left from right, he must be given a great deal of practice in moving his eyes from left to right on the printed page. A crayoned line drawn down the left side of the page will help remind him that he must start to read on that side. An arrow drawn across the page from left to right will help, as will underlining the first letter. Printing the first letter of each word in colored crayon will remind him to sound out from left to right. You will find additional exercises in early grade workbooks.

*If your student has difficulty in learning the letter shapes, remember to use all of his senses in teaching him. This is a common difficulty for young learners who have never advanced beyond the primer or pre-primer level, no matter what grade they are now in. Use cut-out letters. Have the student touch them, or trace them with his fingers, or both. Use different materials for the cut-out letters, such as felt, sandpaper, and velvet. Have him trace them in different textures. Have him shape them out of clay, out of pipe cleaners. Have him combine the letters into words, and say the words.

*Tracing the solid letters and then the broken letters
will help the student learn the letter shapes.*

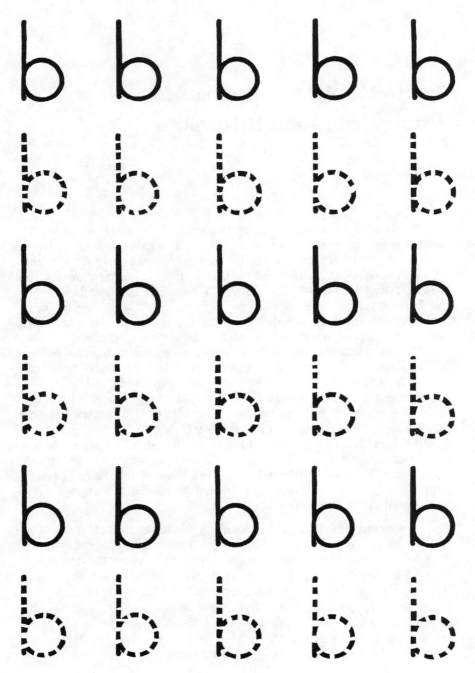

WHAT TO DO ABOUT COMMON READING ERRORS AND DIFFICULTIES

*If your student reverses words or letters, or reads them backwards, he is actually failing to read from left to right. This is so common a problem among backward readers that it requires special attention. Patient practice in sounding out letters in sequence from left to right will usually solve this difficulty. Words most frequently reversed are: saw, was, on, no not, ton, pot, top, now, won.

*If your student guesses and substitutes words, he may be reading material that is too difficult for him. Give him easier material to read. Although he will probably still guess, his guesses and substitutions will be fewer. Be patient; stop him, and urge him to sound out his words; however, try not to stop him too frequently. On occasion, when the substitution does not substantially alter the meaning of the material, it may be overlooked in order to add fluency to the reading.

*If your student omits words and letters, he is not yet reading smoothly. His eye may skip a word now and then, and he does not read phrases well enough to absorb all of the words; this is similarly true when he skips letters within a word. Such errors should be called to his attention as they occur; as his skill and fluency increase, this problem should disappear. Practice in reading phrases, so that the eye takes in several words at each stop, will help in overcoming this difficulty. Suggestions for teaching the reading of phrases are on pages 159-165.

*If your student reads word by word, as though the words were in a list, he still finds each new word a difficult problem and is not yet able to read phrases, nor to comprehend easily what he is reading. The mechanics of reading are still a problem to him. This student needs practice in reading phrases and in reading with expression. The teacher should expose one phrase at a time in the reading matter so that the student is encouraged to read the whole phrase, and then move on to the next. Most important is to give the student confidence in his ability to read, to give him practice in oral reading, and to help him relax. With increased skill and relaxation, his oral reading will become expressive and less mechanical.

*If, during silent reading, your student forms the word with his lips, he will have difficulty learning to read quickly. Explain to him that he must not say the words when he is reading them. Let him hold a pencil in his mouth while reading silently, to prevent the lip motion.

*If your student repeatedly loses his place while reading, let him hold a ruler or a piece of paper under the line he is reading. After a while, try removing it. If he still loses his place, let him continue the use of the line guide. Remove it when he no longer needs it.

*If your student confuses letters, such as, b — d; p — q; t — f — l; m — w; u — n; h — n; point out the slight differences between the pairs. In most cases, he is confusing letters that have the same shape, but face in different directions. In other cases (as h and n) the differences between the shapes of the two letters is very slight. In the case of letters that have the same shapes, as b and d, and p and q, the letters should be printed large, and traced. The direction in which each points should be emphasized. Try to give concrete associations to the shape of each letter. For example, b and d have flagpoles, which p and q have long tails; b has a big belly; d is a doll or a duck; p is like pulling a church bell down; m has two mountains. Associate key words with each letter. Make use, too, of the sensory aids suggested in the section on learning letters.

Exercises like the following are helpful. Have the student circle every **b.**

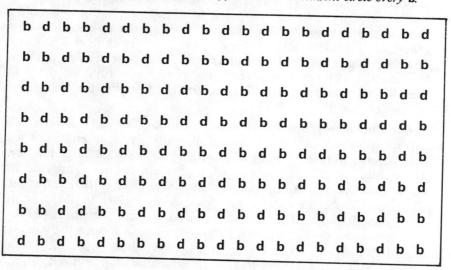

*If after you have pointed out the differences, he continues to confuse a particular pair of letters, follow this procedure: teach him one of the letters, temporarily ignoring the second. Concentrate on the first letter until he knows it automatically. At this point, introduce the second letter, setting aside the first one; teach the second one until he knows it very well. Now bring back the first, and let him work on both letters together. Though he may still, for a short time, confuse them slightly, he will quickly learn to discriminate between the two.

Sample Lesson Plan

LESSON PLAN				
STUDENT Jimmy Jones (Beginning Reader) LESSON _____				
DATE _____ TEACHER _____				

GOALS FOR TODAY	ACTIVITIES	TUTOR'S COMMENTS	NEXT LESSON	SUPERVISOR'S COMMENTS
1. Learn Sight Words.	Play game: Go Fish.	Went well.	Play this game again.	
2. Review sounds of short vowels a, i.	Use sound out sheets.	Needs more drill on i. Knows a.	i	
3. Learn short vowel u.	Use sound out sheets.	Is still hesitant.	u	
4. Develop comprehension.	Discuss TV show tutor and student saw last night.	He needs encouragement to speak.	Assigned same show for next week. Remember to discuss it.	
5. Combine 1 and 4 above.	Student dictates a story for Write-Your-Own Book, based on discussion in 4.	Dictation went well. He cannot read many of the words.	Practice these words before attempting to reread story.	
6. Enjoyment of reading.	Read from newspaper a human-interest story.	Picked the wrong story. Not interesting to the student.	Try something related to flying. Seems interested in that.	

Above is a sample lesson plan which a tutor has prepared for his work with a student who recognizes only a few words at sight, and is learning how to sound out words. At present, this student can sound out a number of the consonant sounds, and has just learned the sounds of the short a and i. Notice that the tutor has prepared for six different activities within the one session. The lesson includes something old (review of short vowels a and i); something new (short vowel u); an opportunity for the student to discuss something interesting to him, thereby improving his use of spoken language. During the period when he dictates a story to the teacher, the student is encouraged to use his own interests as a means of developing reading matter. He is given an opportunity to relax and derive pleasure from written material, when the teacher (6) reads a brief selection to him.

The tutor has set clear and simple goals for the lesson. He is not always successful in his choice of material, or in his approach. The notes he makes in columns 3 and 4 are invaluable guides in remembering what should be done at the next lesson. The supervisor's comments in the last column from time to time can assist greatly in planning the tutoring.

STUDENT PROGRESS RECORD

Child _____ Age _____ School _____ Grade _____ Tutor _____

	SEPT.	OCT.	NOV.	JAN.	FEB.	MAR.	APR.	MAY	JUNE
Date of First Entry: 197									

Note: *In the first column place a + next to each skill that the student has at the beginning of instruction, or at the beginning of the school year. In each monthly column mark with a check those skills on which you are working. When the student has mastered that skill, mark a + in that month's box.*

I. DIRECTIONALITY:

Knows left and right 6 times out of 6

II. WORD RECOGNITION AND WORD ATTACK SKILLS

1. Sight Vocabulary (indicate number of words student knows)

2. His own sight words

3. Gaps in phonic knowledge:

(Circle in red the sounds the student knows at the beginning. In the monthly columns, list the sounds you are working on that month. As the student learns a sound thoroughly, circle the appropriate letter on the printed list with a color other than red.)

a. Consonants: d, f, h, j, k, l, m. n, p, q, r, s, t, v, w,
x, y, z
Hard c, g; soft c, g

b. Consonant blends: bl, br, pl, cl, fl, gl, sl, pr, cr, fr,
gr, tr, dr, sp, st, sc, sk, sm, sw, sn, tw

c. Digraphs: sh, eh, th, ph, wh

d. Short vowels: a, e, i, o, u

e. Long vowels: a, e, i, o, u

f. Additional vowel combinations and sounds: ee, ea, oo, oi, ow, ar, ir, ur, oa, ai, au, av, or, er, ov, ou, igh, aw, ay, ew

4. Recognizes

a. Prefixes: en, ex, in, pre, con, com, de, dis, pro, re, un

b. Endings: ing, ed, er, est, ance, ous, able, ent, ant, al, ive, ly, ness, ment, tion, ful

III. COMMON PROBLEMS:

Place a check mark next to each of the problems that your student has. Note that if he is totally unable to read words and sentences, the first 10 items on this list may not apply to him.

1. Word by word reading
2. Monotone: lack of meaningful inflection
3. Ignores punctuation
4. Phrasing poor
5. Repetitions
6. Hesitations
7. Very slow
8. Too rapid
9. Loses place
10. Makes substitutions
11. Reversals

Normal Sequence for Acquisition of Reading Skills

The skills listed here are usually introduced at the grade level designated at the right of each; the grade may vary slightly in some school districts. Each skill is reinforced and taught at a more advanced level, during each succeeding grade.

ANALYSIS OF SOUNDS IN WORDS

	LEVEL
Left to right eye movements	Reading-readiness
Recognizing rhyming words	Reading-readiness
Recognizing consonant sounds	Reading-readiness
Associating consonant sounds with letters	First
Associating short vowel sounds with letters	First
Reading long vowel sounds	First
Blending consonant and vowel sounds	First
Recognizing, when seen and when heard, consonant blends that represent two sounds: bl, br, cl, cr, dr, dw, fl, fr, gl, gr, pl, pr, sc, sk, sl, sm, sn, sp, st, sw, tr, tw, scr, str	Second
Recognizing consonant combinations that represent one sound: sh, th, wh, ch, ph, ng, gh	Second
Recognizing vowel combinations: ee, ea, oo, aw, ew, ow, oi, oy, ou, oa, ai, ay	Second
Recognizing vowel sounds with r: ar, er, ir, or, ur	Second

ANALYSIS OF WORD STRUCTURE

Recognizing root words	First
Forming plurals by adding s, es, ies	First
Recognizing compound words	Second
Adding common suffixes to roots	Second
Adding common prefixes to roots	Second
Recognizing contractions	Third
Recognizing possessives	Third
Dividing words into syllables	Third
Recognizing the use of accent	Fourth

COMPREHENSION SKILLS

Beginning instruction in reading focuses on two aspects simultaneously: mastery of the mechanical aspects of reading, and comprehension. After the mechanical aspects of reading have been mastered, comprehension skills are further developed through increased understanding and use of the printed page. Reading instruction from this point on concentrates on helping the student understand and interpret what he reads.

Understanding and Interpreting Meaning

Each of the following processes and skills is involved in the comprehension of written matter:

- Understanding literal meaning of words, sentences, selections
- Understanding the meaning of punctuation marks
- Relating the story, telling what happened first, what happened then, and what happened last
- Getting the main thought
- Finding details
- Following instructions
- Seeing relationships and making comparisons
- Predicting outcomes and solutions
- Understanding meaning of figurative language
- Drawing conclusions
- Making generalizations
- Seeing cause and effect

Critical Reading

In order to read with discrimination, the student should have guidance and practice in the following:

- Distinguishing the significant from the trivial, relevant from irrelevant, fact from opinion
- Evaluating material read from the reader's own experience and from other criteria
- Determining the writer's point of view
- Reading widely on controversial issues
- Maintaining an objective and inquiring point of view

STUDY SKILLS

Many who read well are unfortunately unable to use their reading to learn. They therefore require instruction and practice in the following study skills.

- Alphabetizing

- Locating Information through the use of
  the title page and table of contents
  maps, diagrams
  the glossary and index
  the dictionary
  the encyclopedia and other reference materials
  graphs and tables
  the bibliography
  the library catalog

- Organizing Information
  listing
  classifying
  finding main ideas
  selecting important details
  skimming to find specific information
  summarizing
  outlining
  note-taking
  rereading to aid in retention

  Learning How to Study
  note-taking
  outlining
  reviewing
  anticipating questions and formulating answers

- Committing Information to Memory
  practicing, with intervals between each practice or study period.
  continuing to practice until the response is automatic

- Test-Taking
  overviewing the test
  judging how to allocate time for each question
  making judgment of whether guessing is penalized on this
  particular test.

How to Prepare an Outline for a Report

I. **Introduction:** Many students are overwhelmed by an assignment to prepare a report, even though they possess the competence and technical skills to read the required material, to gather the necessary information, and to organize it properly. They need guidance in how to prepare an outline. An outline is an orderly arrangement of ideas and information. It helps to clarify ideas and to facilitate their recall by establishing relationships among them. The outline may be sketchy or detailed, depending on how it is to be used.

II. **Purpose:**
   A. To organize ideas and information for study and recall.
   B. To organize ideas and information for the preparation of a written report or an oral presentation.

III. **Procedure:**
   A. Preparation
      1. In preparing an outline of material that the student hears, he must take notes and then treat those notes as though they were reading matter.
      2. To prepare an outline of material that he reads, the student should first skim the selection to get an overview of it, and then read the selection carefully, outlining it as he reads it. See below for further instructions.
      3. To prepare an outline for a written or oral presentation that he will make, the student should list his thoughts, ideas and facts in a legible fashion. He should then reorganize them into an outline.

      Sometimes it is helpful if the teacher or the tutor asks leading questions to encourage the student in expressing his thoughts and ideas.

   B. Preliminary Thinking About Ideas and Details
      1. Identify the central theme.
      2. Identify the main ideas.

3. Identify the details that support the main ideas.
   a. Sometimes they illustrate the main idea.
   b. Sometimes they explain the main idea.
   c. Sometimes they give reasons for or causes of the main idea.
   d. Sometimes they give chronological or sequential development of events of the main idea, or relating to the main idea.
   e. Sometimes they give definitions of the main idea.
4. Identify the relationships among the ideas.

C. Writing the Outline
   1. Organize the facts and ideas according to
      a. Sequence, or
      b. Importance, or
      c. Any relationship that you have selected
   2. Insert supportive details (or facts) in the appropriate section, according to the organization you have selected.
   3. Consolidate outline by
      a. Combining ideas that are similar
      b. Discarding minor or inconsequential details
      c. Discarding irrelevant thoughts or data
      d. Avoiding repetition.

   4. Form of the Outline
      a. To indicate parallel and subordinate relationships easily, it is helpful to use a combination of letters and numerals in outlining.
         i.   Roman Numerals — main thoughts or ideas
         ii. Capital letters — major details
         iii. Arabic Numerals — minor details
         iv. Lower Case Letters — subordinate details.
      b. Subheadings may be added to clarify the meanings of headings.
      c. Each item is indented according to its importance. All listings of the same letter or numeral carry parallel indentation and similar weight or value in terms of their relationships within the outline.

Sound-Out Lists

Where to Find Sound Out Lists

Consonants
THAT ALWAYS
SOUND THE SAME

b
d
f

h
j
k
l

m
n
p
r

s
t
v

w
x
z

b b	n n
d d	p p
f f	r r
h h	s s
j j	t t
k k	v v
l l	w w
m m	x x
z z	

93

Sound-Out Lists

These words lists may be used in a number of ways to provide drill in teaching how to sound out words. Several suggestions follow.

1. Present the lists to your student directly from this manual. In order to show the student only one word at a time, cut a small window out of an index card and frame the word in this space.

2. Rewrite the words, as you need them, on index cards or on cardboard sheets. Use a felt-tipped pen; make each word large and clear, leaving space between the lines so that each word stands out clearly.

3. If you write each word on a separate card, the words may be used as flash cards. Be careful to present them to the student slowly at first.

4. Word wheels and other devices help to vary your presentations and add interest and novelty to the instruction (see pages 159-163).

5. Present the words in varied order. Remember that you want the student to *sound out* the words, not to memorize them.

6. Remember that the student needs a great deal of practice. If necessary, find more words.

Short a

sat	pan	can	an	rat
ban	bat	ram	mad	bag
pat	sap	man	Sam	tap
bad	am	map	sad	cab
mat	dad	had	lad	jab
ham	ran	tan	pad	jam
fat	rag	dam	rap	tag
sag	hat	fan	has	fad
pal	lap	add	at	gap

Short i

is	rid	it	sit	wit	win
hip	hid	rib	fit	dig	rip
his	him	did	hit	dip	fig
tin	sill	lid	fib	wig	dim
bill	rim	nip	tip	bid	bib
sip	in	big	sin	till	fin
lip	miss	ill	bit	mill	jig

Review of Short Vowels **a** and **i**

mill	pan	dad	hid	pin	nap
rib	kit	pat	till	dim	ham
him	ran	bad	tap	had	fit
map	kill	hip	ran	rap	did
hit	bat	am	sin	bat	bib
lip	fat	lid	fib	will	dam

Short **U**

hub	but	us	hum	nut	fun
hut	rub	pup	dug	up	rug
sun	bud	mud	gum	nun	sup
bun	cub	tub	hub	rum	gun
jut	tug	bug	cud	bum	cut
run	bus	sub	rut	sum	hug

Review of Short a, i and u

sun	mill	mud	fat	bad	rut
rib	bud	pan	kid	rub	man
kill	jut	bat	hat	sub	hid
till	map	bun	hut	ran	win
run	fib	sin	us	dim	cub
had	lug	rap	did	sup	bun
bib	hub	dam	tub	bus	ran

Short e

red	men	mess	bed	fez	wed
net	pet	get	well	peg	less
den	jet	bet	Ben	Tess	vet
hen	wet	bell	let	fed	tell
led	keg	hem	pen	hep	set
ten	beg	Ned	fell	met	Meg
set	pep	Ted	sex	sell	leg

Review of Short Vowels a, i, u, and e

fell	ban	dug	less	kiss	den	tan
tell	hut	tub	hub	kid	tap	kill
ten	pet	dim	bun	sun	tag	had
bid	led	pen	mud	till	rib	sit
let	but	fed	sub	mill	bat	Ben

Short o

odd	hop	dot	lot	doll	rob
mob	hot	cob	hop	fog	top
pot	rot	job	not	cot	lop
nod	Tom	fob	pop	bob	sop
pod	sob	mop	cod	got	mod
rod	hod	sod	mom	tot	hog

Review of All Short Vowel Sounds

jam	get	will	rod
red	is	mob	sun
fin	add	wet	rot
jet	pot	run	mud
not	rob	sob	web
bud	bus	bad	dog
rat	bet	hot	jut
his	tap	hen	pup
lip	sin	well	man
pet	us	bed	tin
hut	bid	win	pan
web	bat	sap	pod
tub	hum	hip	sod
fan	mad	bun	dad
top	net	tip	bill

Consonants

c as in

cat	cap	cod	can
cot	cub	cud	cuff

c as in

cigar	center	cell	civil	cement
cent	cigarette	city	cellar	cereal

g as in

goat	go	gob	gal	gap
gut	got	gag	gum	girl

g as in

giraffe	gee	ginger	George	gender
gem	gin	gentle	general	giant

q as in

queen	quill	queer	quack	quarter
quit	quiz	quip	quick	question

y as in

yo-yo	yet	yap	yak	yard	your
yellow	yam	yes	yell	year	you

Long Sounds of Vowels

RULE: When you see "o" at the end of a word, the "o" has a long sound.

no	so	go	ho	yo-yo

RULE: When two vowels are together, name the first vowel and skip the second.

ee

deep	feel	peep	beet	deem	beef	weep
deer	see	keel	heed	reel	fee	jeer
need	meek	deep	feet	seed	weed	leek
peel	reek	keep	reed	heel	week	keen
lee	seen	feed	seem	wee	reef	bee

ay

say	bay	hay	way	may	nay	lay
jay	day	ray	pay	gay	play	stay

ai

nail	pail	vain	bail	laid	hair	wait
main	gait	bait	mail	maid	hail	pair
lain	tail	raid	gain	paid	rail	jail
fail	fain	pain	fair	sail	maim	wail
rain	gain	wait	bait	lair	waif	aim

102 *SOUND OUT LISTS*

Double Vowels

ea

beat	neat	bead	tea	veal	peak	meal
team	hear	bean	mean	beak	heal	wean
meat	eat	ear	seal	read	leaf	beam
deal	leak	leap	real	near	seam	fear

oa

oat	load	roam	foam	goad	oak	road
goat	boat	road	coat	load	soap	oaf
goal	foal	toad	loaf	moan	soak	oar
coal	loan	hoax	moat	coax	roan	loam

ie

lie	pie	die	tie	lied	tried	cried

ue

hue	sue	rue	due	true	blue	clue

oe

doe	foe	Joe	Poe	toe	woe

Double Vowels (Mixed)

nail	wait	sue	suit	seen	hue	wheel
meat	deal	aim	sea	soap	mail	load
oak	due	leaf	pie	neat	week	beat
need	deep	feet	eat	foe	hear	teem
team	chair	foam	roar	died	tie	leak

The Silent "e"

RULE: When you see a vowel-consonant-final "e" combination, name the first vowel and skip the "e". The final "e" is silent.

make	mine	ate	sale	file	pure	mile
zone	line	made	cure	mate	cute	lake
bode	lane	hole	male	rave	fine	kite
tube	cake	bone	life	page	use	nine
ripe	pole	bite	time	mole	cape	rise
dote	dine	sole	same	bale	mice	cope
poke	pale	fuse	five	race	dome	bake
ride	mane	date	coke	vine	hike	dive
pine	cane	tune	tide	hate	rope	gale

Review of Short and Long Vowel Sounds

ripe	hop	fin	set	met	ran	goat
pad	hate	paid	bead	pine	not	tape
use	men	rob	neat	cub	rod	bed
bet	did	rode	can	pin	rid	tube
got	gape	mean	rip	lad	rain	died
pain	cane	dim	hat	mad	dime	tub
beat	pan	cute	rate	made	ate	cube
win	us	bait	robe	man	wine	meat
pet	rat	hope	laid	pane	road	cut

Consonant Combinations

pl	cl	bl	fl	gl
play	clock	blue	flee	glue
plow	claim	blade	flame	glass
plan	club	bless	flag	glee
plight	clang	bluff	flit	gleam
plea	clean	blank	fleet	glow
plume	clip	blink	flea	gloom
plank	clap	black	flute	glide
plain	clot	bleat	fled	glen
plane	clean	blond	flour	glean
plate	clear	bled	flog	glib
plait	clash	bleed	flick	glum
plant	clay	blood	flight	glint
plot	clam	blend	flare	glimmer
please	Clark	blare	fly	glove
plum	clerk	blunt	flask	glaze
pluck	click	blurt	flirt	glare
pleat	claw	block	fling	glad
ply	clod	blind	flint	glade
plod	clump	blame	flesh	
	clove	blaze	flash	
		bleak		
		blade		

Consonant Combinations

sl	pr	cr	fr	br
slide	print	cram	fresh	bred
slave	proof	cream	friend	bread
slid	prove	crib	frank	braid
slope	pride	crane	from	broke
slap	prune	creep	fray	brink
sleep	preach	crack	free	brand
slept	print	crush	frame	brake
slip	prick	crop	frill	break
slay	prism	crab	fright	bring
sleet	prop	cry	fringe	brought
sleigh	prize	crisp	frog	brother
sled	price	crust	fry	bride
sleeve	press	cramp	frock	brood
sloop	prod	crag	frond	brush
slight	prim	crash	frisky	brand
slinky	pram	craft	fret	breech
sloppy	pretty	crazy	freak	branch
slur	proud	crease	freeze	brunch
sling	pray	creek	frail	brick
	praise	crime	France	brown
	pry	crimp	frail	broil
			froth	brim

Consonant Combinations

gr	tr	dr	sp	st
grand	true	drive	spell	stand
gray	tree	dress	span	still
greet	track	dream	spit	stain
groan	trick	drill	spat	stone
gruff	train	drink	speck	stop
graze	truck	drank	spill	stay
grass	trunk	drunk	speak	stall
green	tram	drab	speech	stake
grief	trade	drag	spin	steak
grape	trail	drake	spine	stack
greed	tramp	drape	spark	stag
grill	trap	draw	spank	stab
gripe	trash	drawn	spunk	stage
grit	tray	dry	spade	stalk
grin	treat	drip	spawn	stem
grime	trip	drop	spent	start
grim	trill	droop	spun	stark
grab	tripe	drool	spike	star
grout	try	drove	spool	steam
grog	troop	drive	spooky	stamp
ground	trace	drag	spot	stint

Consonant Combinations

sc	sk	sm	sw	sn
scant	skinny	small	swim	snake
scat	skate	smell	sway	sneer
scold	skin	smile	sweep	snatch
scowl	skill	smart	swell	snitch
score	ski	smack	sweet	snug
scoop	sky	smite	swoon	snow
scan	skit	smock	swing	snoop
scale	skid	smog	swank	sneak
scat	skunk	smut	swear	snide
scum	sketch	smug	sweat	snip
scar	skew	smash	swat	snap
scour	skim	smoke	sworn	snack
scarf	skip	smith	swung	snag
scare	skirt	smooth	swoop	snarl
scan	skull	smother	swift	sniff
scalp		smear		snood
scout		smudge		snort
				snore
				snub

Consonant Combinations

tw	spl	spr	str	st
twain	split	spry	strip	fast
twine	splash	sprout	stripe	most
twist	splinter	spring	string	worst
tweet	spleen	spruce	strung	last
twig	splint	sprint	strand	feast
twin	splice	sprang	strike	boast
twill	splurge	spray	struck	toast
twice		sprite	strain	yeast
twirl		sprig	street	first
tweed		sprat	straight	burst
tweak		sprawl	strait	coast
twang		spree	strange	least
twelve			strap	blast
twenty			straw	cast
twitch			stray	mast
			streak	past
			strong	lost
			strife	lust
			stretch	must
			stroke	host

Consonant Combinations

nk	ng	nt	nd
frank	bang	want	friend
bank	sang	bent	band
tank	sing	sent	bend
shrank	wing	lent	wind
drank	swing	gent	wand
Hank	bring	bunt	sand
plank	spring	brunt	send
prank	sprang	blunt	lend
rank	fling	plant	spend
sank	flung	plaint	blond
spank	rung	runt	stand
thank	cling	slant	strand
yank	ding	faint	brand
ink	king	count	grand
think	ping	mount	gland
blink	sling	ant	blend
link	sting	chant	mend
pink	string	grant	spend
skunk	thing	pant	trend
spunk	wrung	hint	tend
junk		lint	blind

Additional Drill
on
Consonant Combinations

drive	stay	glow	fling	dress	breach
prowl	flight	sleeve	crab	blunt	tray
swim	groan	smite	plait	true	frail
skill	bring	slow	pluck	swing	spool
clash	twig	crop	grip	sneer	skirt
frock	scant	glass	trail	snack	gleam
plate	plank	blond	press	brag	drug
snake	sweep	smell	skate	still	spank
train	graze	bright	gray	free	crib
drip	scab	stand	truck	crush	bless
strike	scrub	strive	crisp	skull	tract
grasp	yelp	held	strip	brisk	cleft
milk	gulf	feast	plant	splash	shelf
dump	sprite	sprout	screech	frisk	boast
film	weld	scrap	bulb	grab	belt
cramp	trust	shrink	stress	plaint	dream
spleen	desk	twin	welt	scalp	tramp
twist	trump	flame	stand	ground	crust
stream	waist	split	blot	state	lump
tweed	blend	scum	flour	wilt	smelt
skip	sport	dream	split	slept	flake
stick	scorn	prow	swept	crime	plump

Additional Consonant Sounds

sh

ship	shod	shut	dish	shot
shoe	shin	hash	shop	rash
shelf	show	shed	cash	shell
shift	shave	shore	shun	shake

ch

chick	chip	chop	chin	chit
chug	chat	chest	much	rich
catch	hatch	scratch	pitch	hitch
pinch	patch	ranch	latch	chap

th

thimble	thank	thing	thick	thump
both	with	bath		

and

than	then	them	this	the	that

wh

whale	which	whit	whack	whine
while	wheat	wheel	whet	what
white	whim	whiff	whip	wish

Review of sh, ch, th, and wh

shell	chug	rash	shin	chop	with	both
rich	chin	shelf	chest	fish	thick	chill
shop	chum	hash	this	chin	thin	whim
whip	ship	thing	show	chap	thank	whisk
the	that	them	they	their		

Additional Vowel Sounds

oo

room	soon	roof	cool	drool	broom	food
pool	boot	spool	loop	toot	moon	tool
root	shoot	spoon	hoop	boom	loon	stool
droop	coop	pool	fool	noon	troop	roof

oo

stood	foot	took	good	book	cook	look

oi,oy

boil	soil	join	joy	coil	boy	Roy
toil	point	toy	broil	flow	spoil	coy

ow

cow	owl	plow	gown	hound	stout	now
found	down	how	fowl	round	mound	sound
ground	clown	wow	frown	sour	brow	mouth

ow

low	flow	bow	row	tow	mow	slow
grow	blow	snow	throw	know	glow	crow

aw, au

paw	raw	saw	jaw	straw	shawl	haul
Saul	crawl	claw	yawn	draw	fault	dawn
lawn	Paul	raw	maul	law	flaw	craw

Review of Additional Vowel Sounds

boot	choose	show	boon	stoop	cool	thaw
bloom	food	room	book	shoot	noise	broil
smooth	coin	look	spoil	soot	choice	ouch
grouch	cook	house	joint	loud	frown	poise
shout	mooch	jaw	glow	blouse	raw	tow

Vowels Combined with r

RULE: Vowel sounds are different when they precede *r*.

ar *as in car*

bar	part	cart	bark	mark	car	park
hard	dark	darn	dart	charm	harm	chart
farm	lark	tar	jar	man	barb	barn
lard	tart	yarn	start	yard	march	far

Vowels Combined with r

or *as in horse*

sort	sport	fork	corn	nor	snort	cork
cord	north	short	for	or	born	York

ir *as in sir,* er *as in her,* ur *as in fur*

herd	term	germ	pert	hunter	clerk	birth
curl	fir	third	fur	stir	dirt	sir
teacher	flirt	fern	burn	first	twirl	cur
girl	server	skirt	shirt	church	spur	firm
turn	summer	curve	bird	burr		

all *words*

wall	ball	all	hall	call	stall
fall	small	tall	gall	mall	pall

ight *words*

right	fight	light	sight	might	tight	bright
fright	plight	night	blight	flight	slight	bight

Words That Rhyme

an	at	am	ag	ad	ap	ot
ban	bat	am	bag	add	cap	blot
can	cat	clam	brag	bad	chap	clot
fan	drat	dam	drag	cad	zap	cot
man	flat	ram	flag	dad	clap	dot
pan	slat	jam	gag	fad	gap	knot
plan	fat	ham	hag	gad	lap	got
bran	hat	tram	lag	glad	map	hot
ran	mat	slam	crag	had	nap	jot
tan	gnat	sham	nag	lad	rap	lot
van	pat	scram	rag	mad	sap	not
began	sat		sag	pad	slap	plot
Japan	rat		snag	sad	snap	pot
	vat		tag		strap	rot
			wag		tap	shot
			zigzag		trap	slot
					pap	spot
						tot
						trot
						forgot

Words That Rhyme

ob	it	in	id	ut	un	up	ud
Bob	bit	bin	bid	mut	bun	up	bud
lob	fit	din	did	jut	shun	cup	spud
slob	hit	chin	hid	rut	fun	pup	cud
cob	kit	fin	kid	but	gun	sup	dud
job	knit	grin	lid	cut	run		mud
mob	lit	in	mid	hut	spun		Jud
rob	pit	kin	rid	nut	stun		thud
snob	quit	pin	skid	Tut	sun		
sob	sit	shin	slid	gut	begun		
blob	slit	sin					
	spit	skin					
	split	spin					
	wit	thin					
	flit	tin					
	omit	twin					
		win					
		violin					
		begin					

Words That Rhyme

eed	et	en	ed	old	ay	
heed	bet	Ben	bed	bold	bay	play
deed	get	den	bled	cold	clay	ray
seed	jet	glen	fed	told	day	say
need	let	open	fled	mold	gray	stray
creed	met	hen	led	sold	hay	fray
bleed	net	ken	red	fold	jay	way
reed	pet	men	shed	gold	lay	away
speed	set	pen	sled	hold	May	delay
feed	wet	ten	wed	scold	pay	display
	duet	then		old	pray	fray
		when				

eat

beat	peat		
cheat	seat		
eat	treat		
feat	wheat		
heat	defeat		
meat	pleat		
neat			

eam

steam	beam
gleam	cream
scream	dream
stream	ream
team	seam

eak

weak	streak
beak	squeak
teak	sneak
leak	bleak
speak	creak
peak	freak

Practice in Syllabication

Vowel-Consonant-Consonant-Vowel Combinations

abject	aspen	cartoon	altar	expand
fourteen	bedlam	fender	benzene	blanket
expect	chimney	hostage	cancel	ignore
common	insult	butter	sudden	cordial
suffer	embed	lumber	hello	banter
cottage	traffic	correct	pencil	borrow
costume	attend	banner	barrel	hammer
awful	manner	consult	rescue	attic
plastic	walnut	magnet	cellar	postal
public	begger	carpet	pumpkin	witness
stampede	master	sentence	margin	target
sister	summer	napkin	rabbit	kitten

Practice in Syllabication

Vowel-Consonant-Vowel Combinations

never	present	hotel	broken	story
caper	any	icy	ever	avoid
motel	apart	human	over	ideal
lady	direct	amount	July	August
aware	amuse	holy	female	even
lazy	crazy	tulip	before	baby
tiny	solid			

Additional Practice in Syllabication

committee	cucumber	anticipate	remember
alcohol	abdomen	aggravate	carnival
molasses	amplify	barbecue	important
innocent	entertain	occupy	February
accident	October	November	tomato
December	indirect	September	Halloween
volcano	yesterday	passenger	romantic
domestic	torpedo	carpenter	committee
remainder	surrender	rectify	republic
revolver	establish	advertise	occupant

Compound Words

baseball	airport	tonight	moonlight
bookcase	manpower	forecast	highway
shoestring	schoolboy	milkweed	nightgown
downstairs	godfather	eyelash	understand
snowflake	milkman	outcome	sailboat
broadcast	policeman	careless	mailman
anyone	outside	without	uptown
Sunday	inside	someone	cowhand
football	showcase	cottonseed	housefly
downtown	maybe	hallway	fullgrown
lonesome	anyway	cowboy	sunshine
peanut	bowstring	newsboy	password
schooldays	sidewalk	wallpaper	sidestep
anybody	popcorn	birthday	overcook
lighthouse	upstairs	notebook	airplane
bathroom	someday	seaman	tapdance
newspaper	midnight	grapefruit	handbag
snowball	waterfall	tablecloth	schoolroom
grandmother	godmother	within	afternoon

Prefixes

Sound-Out Beginnings Added To Root Words

Word Wheels are helpful in learning to read these words.
(See pages 159-165)

en	ex	in	pre
enter	examine	include	preschool
entire	external	insert	preview
entrance	expert	income	precede
enlist	expense	intact	precinct
enrage	expel	increase	prefer
ensue	expect	indeed	prefix
enjoy	exit	indoor	prepaid
enlarge	exist	inform	prepare
engulf	exhaust	inhale	present
engage	exhale	insane	pretend
enfold	exercise	inside	prevail
enact	excuse	insight	prevent
enable	except	inspect	prewar
endear	excite	instep	precaution
enforce	exact	insult	preside
enclose	example	intend	predict
enchant	extra	intuition	preliminary
	extreme	inland	

Prefixes

con	com	de	dis
conform	compute	deflate	disown
conceal	compound	debate	disable
convince	compose	degrade	distress
concern	complain	decay	disagree
contact	compete	deduce	dispute
concert	complete	deceive	disarm
conserve	compass	deliver	disrupt
conclude	compare	decide	disband
contract	commit	declare	discard
concrete	commerce	decline	discharge
contain	comfort	decrease	disclose
consume	comment	deduct	discount
construct	combine	defeat	discuss
consist	combat	defend	disease
consent	comic	deform	disgust
connect	comma	delay	dislike
confuse	common	demand	dismiss
		delight	distrust

Prefixes

pro	re	un
protest	redo	unsure
provoke	recall	unprepared
protect	relearn	unwashed
propose	receive	undone
pronoun	remain	unclear
promote	record	unusual
program	reduce	unhappy
profile	remove	unfold
produce	report	unfit
procure	respect	unfair
proceed	reform	uneasy
proclaim	replace	undress
proportion	retire	uncut
	reward	uncover
	regain	uncommon
	refresh	unclean
	reproduce	unborn
	resort	unarmed

Suffixes

Sound-Out Endings Added To Root Words

(These lists can be used in making word wheels and devices described on pages 159-165.)

s	ing	ed	er	est
helps	helping	helped	taller	tallest
asks	asking	asked	shorter	shortest
calls	calling	called	warmer	warmest
cooks	cooking	cooked	smaller	smallest
bumps	bumping	bumped	older	oldest
kicks	kicking	kicked	harder	hardest
pays	paying	payed	newer	newest
pulls	pulling	pulled	longer	longest
starts	starting	started	lighter	lightest
thanks	thanking	thanked	kinder	kindest
wants	wanting	wanted	colder	coldest
talks	talking	talked	cleaner	cleanest
works	working	worked	blacker	blackest
adds	adding	added	sooner	soonest
burns	burning	burned	faster	fastest
barks	barking	barked	stronger	strongest
kills	killing	killed	richer	richest
farms	farming	farmed	plainer	plainest
milks	milking	milked	poorer	poorest
pants	panting	panted	nearer	nearest
stains	staining	stained	weaker	weakest
rests	resting	rested	deeper	deepest
rolls	rolling	rolled	darker	darkest
fails	failing	failed	dearer	dearest
seems	seeming	seemed	softer	softest
hears	hearing		fresher	freshest

Suffixes

ance
distance
clearance
performance
instance
ignorance
finance
entrance
assistance
appearance
allowance
annoyance
abundance
reliance

ous
gracious
infamous
glorious
poisonous
nervous
previous
murderous
mountainous
marvelous
joyous
famous
enormous
dangerous

able
table
probable
likeable
remarkable
fashionable
enjoyable
suitable
desirable
dependable
comfortable
considerable
capable
agreeable
available

ent
complement
supplement
defendent
present
permanent
intelligent
innocent
incident
resident
excellent
different
content
comment
dissident

al
mechanical
practical
renewal
refusal
political
musical
electrical
terminal
horizontal
vertical
central
carnival
brutal

ant
servant
merchant
instant
important
ignorant
distant
constant
applicant
accountant
redundant
pennant

ive
extensive
protective
native
adjective
locomotive
impressive
fugitive
expensive
selective
effective
destructive
captive
active

Suffixes

ly	ness	ment	tion	ful
suddenly	business	achievement	vacation	lawful
friendly	easiness	pavement	objection	skillful
sadly	lowness	movement	donation	restful
quietly	tallness	investment	destruction	powerful
gently	whiteness	shipment	exception	peaceful
justly	softness	treatment	correction	painful
yearly	highness	excitement	construction	joyful
highly	greatness	enlargement	connection	harmful
weekly	darkness	engagement	collection	handful
hardly	dampness	deportment	carnation	grateful
warmly	plainness	contentment	attraction	frightful
gladly	sweetness	betterment	adoption	faithful
sweetly	madness	assignment	ration	cupful
freshly	illness	appointment	motion	cheerful
softly	likeness	amusement	action	bashful
freely	sadness	amazement		awful
richly	weakness	agreement		
poorly	goodness			
fairly	sickness			
deeply				
plainly				
closely				
nearly				
openly				
lovely				

Alphabet Key Words

EXAMPLES OF THE SAME LETTER IN DIFFERENT TYPE FACES

Manuscript - small letters	a b c d e f g h i j
Roman - small letters	a b c d e f g h i j
Manuscript - capital letters	A B C D E F G H I J
Roman - capital letters	A B C D E F G H I J

k l m n o p q r s t u v w x y z
k l m n o p q r s t u v w x y z
K L M N O P Q R S T U V W X Y Z
K L M N O P Q R S T U V W X Y Z

131

PART 4

Teaching Reading To Students
To Whom English
Is A Foreign Language

Teaching Reading to Students
To Whom English Is a Foreign Language

For many of your students, English is a second language. Their native tongue may be Spanish, Navajo, Turkish, Italian, or perhaps Indian. Some understand no English at all, while others may understand much of what they hear, may speak haltingly, and yet may be unable to read. Some are recently arrived immigrants and some live in communities where only their native language is spoken, and English is regarded as a strange tongue. They may be of all ages: school children, adolescents, adults, or old people.

Before such students can be taught to read English, they must acquire some listening and speaking skills in this language. The first phase of instruction therefore must concentrate on the acquisition of oral language skills; these include the development of vocabulary and the ability to hold a conversation.

WHAT THE TEACHER SHOULD KNOW
ABOUT THE STUDENT'S WORLD

The number of non-English-speaking children and adults in our schools is large. Since English is a foreign language for them, their problems in learning it are quite special. The teacher or tutor requires an unusual background of information, and enormous understanding and sensitivity in order to be able to assist the non-English-speaking student to learn. Because the student's task is so much more difficult (that is, he must learn to speak a second language before or while he learns to read it), it is harder for him to remain interested in his work. With such students, it is a greater challenge to the tutor to nurture and stimulate the student's interest in learning.

You will have to know a good deal about the world of the student, and how it contrasts with your own. You will be unable to understand the student's behavior and his responses unless you know about his culture and values — his habits and routines, his family ties, what is considered important or unimportant, what behaviors are considered proper and commendable, and those that are considered bad or even unimportant.

You will have to accept and tolerate cultural and value differences, though you may feel very keenly and with great conviction about your own background and values. You must understand that your student grew and developed his behavior patterns in a different environment from your own, and was surrounded by different cultural practices. Now that the student has been transplanted into what is for him, a strange world, his values may change, as may yours as well. But these changes must be a natural result of the exchange between student and tutor. The tutor may not sit in judgment of the student's world. The differences must be accepted and tolerated, and through them, you, the tutor, can indeed gain insights into the student and his behavior through your growing knowledge of his culture.

Let us examine several cultural patterns that may differ. Though these illustrations will probably not relate to any one of your students, they demonstrate how important it is to reserve judgment when the student's behavior is somewhat disconcerting or distressing. Upon further study, you may find that such behavior can be interpreted as completely acceptable, when viewed in terms of the student's cultural background.

Some illustrations may make the contrasts more clear:

1. Punctuality is very important in mainstream American industrialized society. In warmer climates, with less seasonal contrasts in temperature, and in places where there is little

industry, people have tended to have less regard for punctuality than have those in our highly mechanized society. Though inconvenience may result when a student is late for an appointment, the tutor must be able to recognize that this apparently cavalier attitude towards time may be part of a cultural pattern, and is not intended to be a personal affront.

2. Sex roles in many countries are often more sharply contrasted than in the United States. Quite often the male is the absolute head of the group. He makes decisions while the female is usually more passive. The man earns the living for the family; the woman takes care of the home. In preparation for the adult roles, the child's play anticipates the expected adult behavior: boys must not play sissy games; girls may not play rough games. Although these patterns are changing, the cultural contrasts in sex roles remain striking.

3. In some cultures, cooperation has received greater stress than has competition. When students who have been taught cooperation as a way of life take examinations, it would seem natural for them to share their answers freely. In a competitive society, such sharing is frowned upon, and is called "cheating." If the student is to succeed, or even survive, in a competitive society, it is possible that he will have to be taught to compete. However, it will first be necessary to understand his behavior (the sharing of answers on tests must be seen as the result of his cooperative background, rather than as a sign of dishonesty).

The importance of accepting and understanding cultural differences cannot be stressed enough, for as a result of these conflicts, many children of minority groups have poor self-esteem, are embarrassed about the contrast between language spoken at home and that at school, and puzzled about the contrast between behavior expected at home and at school (those we call cultural differences). Their language problems frequently contribute to their school failures, compounding their lack of self-esteem. The sensitive teacher, the sensitive tutor, can counteract this feeling of inadequacy, and can help pave the way to success for the student.

To teach the student successfully, the teacher must try to understand, and not disparage, the student's values and cultural differences. The teacher will realize that cultural differences have made this country vital and dynamic, and these differences must be appreciated, respected and preserved.

As mentioned above, language is a central feature in the culture of any group. The student who feels isolated in an unfriendly English-speaking world, surrounded by people who look down at those he loves, may feel more comfortable, warmer and loved, speaking only his native language with his own group. He may fail to learn to speak English for these reasons.

You must demonstrate in your behavior and in your speech that you respect your students, that you respect their background and culture, that they are worthy individuals, and that you have confidence in their ability to learn. The finest proof of the tutor's respect for the culture of the student is the tutor's ability to converse with the student in his native language; this skill is invaluable. The tutor who lacks this knowledge can show respect by learning some common words and phrases from the student. This provides a double benefit: the tutor acquires a smattering of a second language and at the same time forms a bond with the student.

WHAT THE TUTOR SHOULD KNOW ABOUT LEARNING SPOKEN AND WRITTEN ENGLISH AS A SECOND LANGUAGE

Learning a second language can be as easy for young children as learning a first language; they learn spontaneously from the language of everyday life. Yet teaching English as a second language in school, when English is the only language spoken in school, is not as successful. Children in school who do not speak English are unable at the same time to learn to read, to learn arithmetic, and all other subjects requiring the English language — thus compounding their failure.

Non-English-speaking students arrive in this country at any time of the year. Therefore, they may be admitted to school at any time of the year, and placed in classes in which the students already know each other, know school routines, and have participated in a certain amount of group learning. The new arrival is a stranger to all of these, and must adjust to the other students, to the routines, and to the curriculum all at the same time. The new student is usually placed in the class appropriate for his age and thus, he will be with other students of his age. Yet some of these new students may have had very little schooling previously. They may come from areas in which educational opportunities were limited, or they may come from the families of migrant workers so that their schooling has been repeatedly interrupted. Some of the older students may be functionally illiterate in their native languages; and some of them may know no English at all. Even among those who have had previous instruction in English, the course of instruction to which they have been exposed differ for all. There has been no uniform curriculum; each student, therefore, knows different things.

The difficulties of learning English have been very well publicized, thus creating the additional barrier of anxiety and fear. Learners who anticipate great difficulty are more likely to meet with failure.

English is a difficult language to learn. As you already know, it is difficult to read English because it is not consistent in its spelling. Thus, after learning how to sound out, the reader must learn a great many exceptions to the usual rules.

Understanding spoken English is equally difficult for the foreign speaker. How will the Navajo, or the Greek, or the Spanish-speaking student translate the following sentences?

> *His head was spinning.*
> *He hit the nail on the head.*

Such idioms are usually translated literally — and immediately lose all meaning. The foreign speaker is confused by a word that has several meanings or by words that sound the same; he frequently selects the inappropriate meaning and loses the sense of the conversation. For example:

> *The king reigned (rained?) for 20 years.*

Some English words and phrases, when pronounced with a foreign accent, sound quite different, and seem to mean something different, thus causing confusion to the listener, and embarrassment to the speaker. For example:

> *under* may sound like *on the*
> *hat* may sound like *hot*
> *it* may sound like *eat*
> *day* may sound like *they*

The speaker who finds himself repeatedly misunderstood may retreat to his own language, and give up his attempts to learn to speak English.

In learning to sound out English, a single letter may represent several different sounds, as does the o in each of the following words: **Tom, hole, of.** The letters **ea** sound quite different in each of these words: **beans, bear, heart.**

Many foreign languages omit personal pronouns, or use them in simplified form. Our pronouns, particularly **he, she, his** and **her,** are therefore very difficult for many to learn correctly.

It is important for you to be completely familiar with the obstacles and problems that the learner must overcome in learning the language; you can thus understand, and with this knowledge guide the student to success, and help him circumvent the obstacles. Despite all of the difficulties enumerated, your student can and will learn if you have confidence that he will learn, and if you follow the guidelines outlined in this section.

GUIDELINES TO TEACHING ENGLISH AS A SECOND LANGUAGE

Motivation, Self-Esteem

It is important to repeat that each learner must feel respected, dignified, and successful as he attempts to learn the English language. Basic to his learning, and as an accompaniment to the instruction, are a pride in his native culture and a continuing sense of unity with his native world, even while entering the new English-speaking world. His self-esteem, and therefore his openness to learning will be enhanced by his knowledge of and pride in his native culture. This pride in self can be strengthened while he learns through the use of materials based on the culture and background of the student. Your neighborhood librarian will help you locate such materials. Look for biographies of heroes of his culture; your student will enjoy these, take pride in them, and maintain his interest in learning.

Remember that, as for all students, motivation and instruction must depend on the student's interests and skills. Use subject matter that will be of interest to a student of his age, and teach him those skills that he lacks. Keep in mind that there is no one best way for all students in all situations. Find the best way for your student.

Specific Language Problems

The student must be encouraged to talk and write and read about himself, his home, his culture, his community, his interests, his wishes, desires, needs and emotions. As his speech develops, he will be ready for reading and writing more quickly. He will thus also be ready to participate in the total learning program more readily.

If the student is in a school in which English is the only language spoken, and the student is never permitted to use or hear his native language while English is relatively strange to him, the student may feel isolated and estranged. It is helpful to converse with him in his native language; do so by learning basic words and phrases from the student. This exchange not only gives the student an opportunity to use his native tongue but it gives him pride in it and in his own ability to impart knowledge to his tutor.

To maintain interest and to encourage communication, simple but real conversations should be encouraged from the first day. The meaning should always be clear to the student; the student should never be asked to repeat, to read or to practice material whose meaning is not clear to him. He should be led to understand the material, by relating it, whenever possible, to his own experience.

Oral practice of new words, phrases, and sentences is essential. Natural conversation is one way of giving the student practice. He is thus able to repeat what he has heard. Good pronunciation is learned most easily by imitation of the tutor or another English speaking person. If the student has difficulty in imitating, or speaks with a heavy accent, remember that your goal is that he speak *under-standably*, not perfectly. If you can understand him, his speech is adequate. Try to limit the number of corrections that you make; you do not want the student to feel unsuccessful. Praise him when you can understand him, and whenever he has overcome an obstacle.

Sometimes a student will have special difficulty with a particular sound: he may say sheep for ship or pin for pen. If his accent or dialect (when he substitutes these sounds) makes it difficult to understand him, you may want to give him practice in saying these sounds correctly. In that case, always practice the sounds as part of words; do not have him practice the sounds in isolation as they lose all meaning for the student in this way.

Children under twelve will learn to speak without an accent more easily than will older learners. If you are teaching a young child, therefore, be confident that your conversations with him in English, and his conversations and play with children of his age at school and in the community, and even his listening to the radio and television, all will contribute to his learning to speak English well and without an accent. Remember never to criticize *an accent, or a dialect*, because you will then be criticizing the child's family and his community in which he is surrounded by accents. When correcting the student, concentrate only on a specific pronounciation, a specific sound used in different words — not the accent or dialect.

In order to be able to speak the language well, the student must have good listening skills. He must be able to hear all the correct sounds, words, and word groups, and understand them in the general context. If he misses the meaning of a word because he mis-heard one of the sounds, or because he does not understand the word, he will then lose much of the material that follows. The tutor must speak and work at the speed most comfortable for the student so that this problem can be avoided. The student must also be able to remember what he heard at the beginning, and throughout the listening period until the end, so that he may have a grasp of the total meaning of the speaker. Conversation helps build listening skills, as does reading to the student material of interest to him.

When you teach your student to speak English, the following information about language will be helpful to you:

Vocabulary may be divided into content words and function words. Content words are those we can see, touch, illustrate. They are names of things (nouns), action words (verbs), and words that describe nouns and verbs (adjectives and adverbs).

Function words are the connecting and other words which have little concrete meaning in themselves, but which make it possible to get the total meaning out of statements. These are prepositions, auxiliaries and conjunctions, such as **and. on, to, the, by, for, but.**

Look at this sentence:

The <u>big brown fox jumped</u> over the <u>beautiful table.</u>

The content words are underlined. Content words are easier to teach and easier to learn when they are very concrete and related to the experience of the learner. The content words in the above sentence are easy to illustrate and easy to explain to the learner. Consider this sentence:

<u>John</u> is very <u>loyal</u> and <u>honest.</u>

In this sentence, the content words loyal and honest are abstract: they are difficult to visualize and difficult to explain.

When you teach the non-English-speaking student, begin by teaching those words which are easiest to illustrate and to visualize, or even to touch, to handle, and to smell. As you set these words into sentences, in your conversations with the student, the function words, **(the, and, but, of, how)** are presented to him naturally. Although these words are more difficult to learn, they will become part of his vocabulary as he learns to converse with you.

Point to objects in the room and name them. Name objects in magazines and in books. Prepare a grab bag of objects; have the student reach in, take them out one at a time, and name them.

Reserve the abstract words until your student is able to converse with you in a relaxed way, and has acquired a useful concrete vocabulary.

You may converse with your student about many things in English: school, his favorite game, how he likes his work, television.

Common expressions, such as **good-bye, hello, how are you, so, well,** must be taught to the student systematically so that he may understand them and also use them

Remember that all of us understand much more of the language than we can use; your student will recognize and understand more words than he is able to incorporate into his own speaking vocabulary.

Be careful not to use contractions at the beginning. Say **I do not** rather than **I don't; will not,** rather than **won't.** Contractions are difficult to learn at the beginning, and tend to confuse the learner.

After he is able to converse comfortably, he will be able to learn the contractions more easily. On p. 153 are some of the common phrases, expressions and categories that are helpful to the student who is learning to speak English.

Remember that some Spanish-speaking students tend to drop their final s sounds. This is a common practice in Puerto Rico, and sometimes the habit is carried over to the English language. Look upon this as part of an old habit, rather than an error. Eventually the student will learn to retain the final s.

The English language has a debt to many other languages; although it is basically of Anglo-Saxon origin, it has borrowed many words from Latin. It has many words in common with many of the native languages spoken by your students. In addition, many languages have recently borrowed English words and made part of their own languages. For example, in French, we find the word *rosbif* (roast beef).

Spanish and English have many words in common. Following are some of the similarities that have been observed*, between Spanish and English, together with illustrations. You can make similar comparisons of English with the native language of any of your students.

1. Some words are exactly the same in English and Spanish. This happens most often with words that end in **or, al,** and **able**.

decimal	general
continental	conductor
formidable	considerable

2. Some words in Spanish are the same as their English equivalents, except that in Spanish they have a final vowel, **a, e,** or **o**.

Spanish	English
aparente	apparent
cosmetico	cosmetic
forma	form
idiota	idiot
inconveniente	inconvenient

---

*"Vocabulary Guide of Cognate Words in Spanish and English," Stanley Krippner, Maimonides Hospital of Brooklyn, New York, 1966.

3. English words ending in **tion** are sometimes the same as Spanish words ending in **cion**.

Spanish	English
donacion	donation
determinacion	determination
graduacion	graduation
mocion	motion
ocupacion	occupation

4. Some words in Spanish can be changed to English by doubling the first, second or last consonant of the word.

ilegal	illegal
mision	mission
mocasin	moccasin

5. Some Spanish words can be changed to English by changing the final letter **a** or **o** in Spanish to **e** in English.

defensia	defense
delicado	delicate
globo	globe
impulso	impulse
medicina	medicine

6. Some Spanish words can be changed to English by changing the final **ia** or **io** in Spanish to **y** in English.

diario	diary
geometria	geometry
infancia	infancy
memoria	memory
monopolio	monopoly

7. Some Spanish words can be changed to English by changing the letters **c** or **to** in Spanish to **ch** and **th** in English.

eter	ether
autor	author
catedral	cathedral
caracter	character
coral	choral

8. In some words, change the Spanish **cia** or **cio** to **ce** in English.

palacio	palace
presencia	presence
servicio	service
silencio	silence
distancia	distance

9. In some words, change the final **fia** or **phia** in Spanish to **phy** in English.

bibliographia	bibliography
topografia	topography
caligrafia	caligraphy

10. In some words, change the final letters **dad** in Spanish to **ty** in English.

variedad	variety
velocidad	velocity
vitalidad	vitality
oportunidad	opportunity
capacidad	capacity
claridad	clarity

Idiomatic expressions can be very confusing to the non-English speaking student. So can words with several meanings. Compound words often have meanings that are astonishing to the foreign ear. On Page 146 are some of the words and phrases that require special attention, if your student is to understand spoken English. You will think of many more examples.

Specific Reading Problems for the Non-English-Speaking Learner

When your student has learned enough of the English language from school and through contact with you to be able to hold simple conversations with you, he is ready to begin to learn to read English. If he already knows how to read his native language, he will learn to read English quickly. In any case, teach him to read — following the guidelines in this manual. Find out what he knows, and, in a systematic way, teach those skills that he lacks. Be patient, be confident, and keep in mind that he has special problems and obstacles to overcome. Provide him with the opportunity for success and pride in his achievement, and both you and he will be rewarded by the progress that you will see.

WORDS THAT CONFUSE
THE NON-ENGLISH-SPEAKING LEARNER

Words that Sound Similar

slick	but	gorilla	reel	son
sleek	butt	guerrilla	real	sun
sink	ball	hear	right	stair
zinc	bell	here	write	stare
quiet	be	hole	rode	there
quite	bee	whole	road	their
ever	by	holy	sale	to
every	buy	wholly	sail	too
				two
umpire	bin	knew		
empire	been	new	seam	waist
			seem	waste
trial	berry	know		
trail	bury	no	see	
			sea	
which	close	lessen		
witch	clothes	lesson	seen	
			scene	
eminent	desert	meet		
imminent	dessert	meat	sell	
			cell	
weather	die	miner		
whether	dye	minor	sent	
			cent	
affect	do	plain	scent	
effect	dew	plane		
		rain	so	
except	fair	reign	sow	
accept	fare	rein	sew	

Compound Words

sawbones	browbeat	farfetched	shorthand
headshrinker	aboveboard	firsthand	shorthanded
sourpuss	beeline	bandwagon	highbrow
knothead	skyscraper	halfhearted	lowbrow
screwball	breakdown	holdover	handout
windbag	checkup	layoff	bottleneck
hothead	dropout	makeup	blackout

Selected List of Idioms that Confuse the Student Who is Learning English as a Foreign Language

A-1	At first blush
Of age	At least
All at once	At one's fingertips
All ears	At one's wits' end
All in	At the top
All in all	Ax to grind
All right	Back number
Apple of one's eye	Back on his feet
Apple-pie order	Back out
As a matter of fact	Back up
As yet	Bad blood
At fault	Bad egg

Bag and baggage

Beard the lion

Beat about the bush

Behind one's back

Below the belt

Beside oneself

Beside the point

Better half

Between the devil and the deep sea

Big hand

Big shot

Birds of a feather

Bite one's head off

Blind date

Blow off steam

Bone to pick

Bosom friends

Break away

Break the ice

Bring home the bacon

Bring to mind

Brush-off

Burn the candle at both ends

Burst into tears

Bury the hatchet

Butt in

By and large

By the skin of one's teeth

By the way

Call up

Carry on

Carry the ball

Catch fire

Catch one's eye

Catch red-handed

Chain smoker

Chalk up

Change hands

Change one's mind

Check in

Check out

Chew the fat

Chin up

Chip in

Chips are down

Close call

Cock and bull story

Come in handy

Cook one's goose

Cool as a cucumber

Count one's chickens before they are hatched

Crack a joke

Cream of the crop

Cry wolf

Dark horse

Dead as a doornail

Dirty look

Do away with

Dog-tired

Doll up

Double-cross

Down to earth

Draw the line

Drop by (drop in)

Drop in the bucket

Drop off

Dutch treat

Eat one's cake and have it too

Eat one's heart out

Eat one's words

Elbow grease

Face the music

Fair and square

Fall apart

Far cry

Farfetched

Feather in one's cap

Feather one's nest

Feel blue

Feel it in one's bones

Fence sitter

Fifty-fifty

Finger in every pot (in every pie)

Fit as a fiddle

Flash in the pan

Fly in the ointment

Fool around

Foot the bill

For a song

Forty winks

From A to Z

Get even with

Get in one's hair

Get in touch with

Get it off your chest

Get on one's nerves

Get the upper hand

Get under one's skin

Get wind of

Ghost of a chance

Give a piece of one's mind

Give in

Give the cold shoulder

Go-getter

Go out of one's way

Go straight

Go to bat for

Go to pot

Half-baked

Halfhearted

Hand-to-mouth

Handle with kid gloves

Have a bone to pick

Have a lot on the ball

Have a screw loose

Have cold feet

Have irons in the fire

Have one's hands full

Have one's heart in one's mouth

Head over heels

Hold back

Hold one's horses

Hold one's tongue

Holding the bag

Hot air

In a nutshell

In clover

In dutch

In one's right mind

In the doghouse

In the nick of time

Jot down

Jump at

Keep house

Keep in touch with

Keep one's head

150 *WORDS THAT CONFUSE THE NON-ENGLISH SPEAKING LEARNER*

Keep the wolf from the door

Kill two birds with one stone

Know the ropes

Ladies' man

Laugh up one's sleeve

Lay off

Leave no stone unturned

Left-handed compliment

Leg to stand on

Lend an ear

Like a fish out of water

Look down on

Lose one's shirt

Make a clean breast

Make a mountain out of a molehill

Make believe

Make ends meet

Make eyes at

Make no bones about

Make one's blood boil

Meet halfway

Monkey around with

Nip in the bud

Nose to the grindstone

Old hand

On its last legs

On the dot

On the whole

Out of the question

Pay through the nose

Play the market

Play with fire

Pull a boner

Pull one's leg

Put one's foot down

Put one's foot in one's mouth

Put two and two together

Queer duck

Raw deal

Right-hand man

Rub someone the wrong way

Run across

Save face

Say a mouthful

Scare the daylights out of

See eye to eye

Skate on thin ice

Slip through one's fingers

Smell a rat

Sneeze at

Split hairs

Step on the gas

Stick one's neck out

Stiff upper lip

Straight from the horse's mouth

Straight from the shoulder

Stretch a point

Strike while the iron is hot

Stuffed shirt

Take the bull by the horns

Talk shop

Talk through his hat

Talk turkey

Through thick and thin

Throw in the sponge

To be of age

Tom, Dick and Harry

Tongue lashing

Turn over a new leaf

Under the weather

Under his thumb

Upset the applecart

White elephant

Win hands down (thumbs down)

HELPFUL COMMON PHRASES, EXPRESSIONS AND CATEGORIES

My name is ———.

I live at ———.

I go to school at ———.

I am in the ——— grade.

My teacher is ———.

My telephone number is ———.

I am thirsty (hungry.)

I do not understand.

Please speak more slowly.

Please repeat.

I do not feel well.

My mother is sick.

I was late because ———.

I was absent because ———.

I must go to the bathroom.

Can we play this game?

Can we read this?

Today is Monday.

How are you?

I am fine, thank you.

Where is ———?

How much is ———?

I am very sorry.

Good morning, sir (miss, madam).

Good afternoon (evening).

Good bye.

I want to eat lunch.

I want a drink of water.

I would like a glass of milk.

The line is busy.

There is no answer.

Who is speaking?

This is ——— talking.

You have the wrong number.

To whom do you wish to speak?

I wish to speak to ———.

I am cold (hot).

Yes

No

Please

Where

Hello

Good-bye

Thank you

Excuse me

Where is ———?

I like cake (bread, milk, fruit, egg).

Where is the toilet (bathroom)?

It is there. It is here.

What is your name?

What is your address?

Where do you live?

Which bus (train) goes to ———?

Did you eat breakfast (lunch, dinner)?

Are you hungry?

What time is it? What time do you have?

It is nine o'clock.

What time does the bus leave?

It is early (late, very early, very late).

I am early (late).

Yesterday (today, tomorrow)

Last night

This afternoon

This morning

What day is today?

Today is November 15.

Today is a beautiful day.

It is hot (cold, cloudy, raining, sunny, windy).

What will be the weather tomorrow?

The sun is shining today.

Categories:

Numbers

Colors

Clothes

Parts of the body

Days of the week

Months of the year

Furniture

Food

Coins

Persons, such as girl, boy, man, woman, child

Family relationships, such as daughter, grandmother, sister

PART 5

Useful Teaching Material

DEVICES AND GAMES FOR TEACHING
THE MECHANICS OF READING

Three by Five Cards

These are the simplest, most flexible, and most easily available of all teaching devices. They can be used

> to print words to be learned, one word on a card;
> for word lists;
> for practice in reading a single sound, prefix, or suffix;
> to encourage smoothness in reading.

For example, you might list on a card five words in which the short vowel sounds become long ones (with the addition of the final e). Near the edge of another small card print an e; Have your student place this second card so that the e adjoins each of the printed words in turn. Ask him to read each word with and without the final e.

Cards can also be used to expose individual words or phrases in order to facilitate smooth reading of textual material. Cut a rectangular slot in an unruled 3 by 5 card to form a window. Determine the size of the window by the number of words you want to expose to the student's view at one time. Slide the card across the text as the student reads.

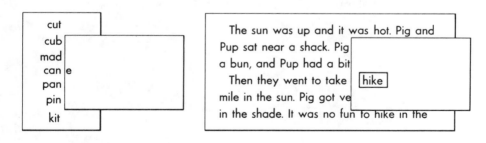

Word Wheels

Word wheels can be used for drill in initial sounds, common word elements, final sounds, prefixes and suffixes. Cut two cardboard circles, one slightly smaller than the other. On the larger wheel, print the required letters. Then cut a slot in the smaller wheel, making sure that it is positioned to expose all of the words in turn as it is rotated. Place the smaller wheel on top and clip them together using a paper fastener.

Thus, for drill in the initial **br**, the upper wheel would read **br** next to the window opening. The lower wheel would show **own, at, eak, ush, ing, ink, ake, ain, ute**.

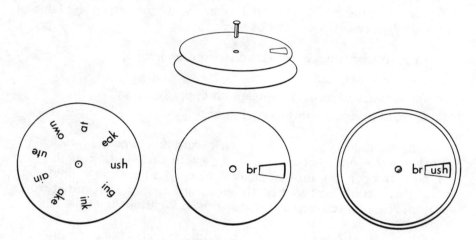

A simple type of wheel can be made of two circular pieces of cardboard, the upper one considerably smaller than the lower one. Sounds to be matched are printed next to the edge of both wheels, so that when the upper wheel is rotated, the sounds on it are matched with the word elements on the outer wheel to form new words.

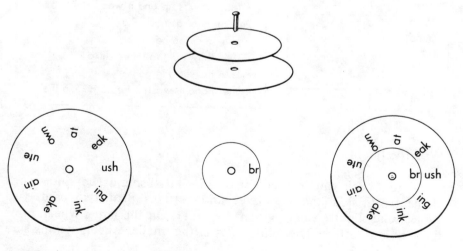

For drill in the use of prefixes and suffixes, a wheel such as shown before can be used. Note that the upper wheel shows a prefix (or a suffix) which appears beside a word-long opening. When the lower wheel (b) is rotated, different base words appear in the opening. These can be read in combination with the prefix (or suffix).

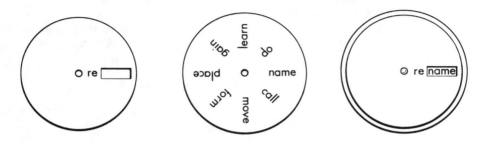

Practice short vowels using a word wheel with two small windows separated by the vowel which is printed on the upper wheel. Appropriate consonants are arranged on the lower wheel so as to form words as the upper wheel is turned.

A wheel with pointers attached with a paper fastener can be used to give the student practice in adding prefixes or suffixes to the words on the wheel.

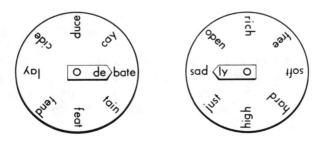

Tachistoscope

This is an effective device for drilling words. Cut a window in a strip of cardboard wide enough to fold into a sleeve 4 inches wide. On another sheet of cardboard, slightly less than four inches wide, print the words that the student is learning. These words should be at least three-quarters of an inch apart and positioned so that they will be exposed through the window one at a time as the inserted card is moved up or down in the sleeve.

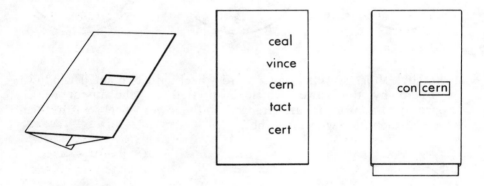

This device may be adapted for use with prefixes or suffixes. In this case, the prefix or suffix is printed on the sleeve next to the window. The base words are printed on the under sheet and exposed one at a time, allowing the student to read with the prefix or suffix added.

Television

In the center of a piece of stiff cardboard, cut two horizontal slits about two inches apart. These slits should be one quarter of an inch from top to bottom and wide enough to permit a two-inch strip of paper to slide through. Adding machine paper is especially suitable for this size opening.

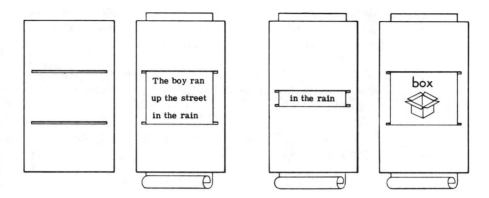

The roll of paper that will pass through the slits should show short printed phrases that tell a story. The paper is pulled slowly through the slits to expose several lines at a time for the student to read.

For younger children, make the opening and the paper strip larger, and illustrate the strip; let the student draw and color the cardboard.

This device can be adapted to help overcome word-by-word reading. For this purpose, use a smaller opening and less space between slits, so that no more than an inch of the strip is exposed at one time. In this practice, which is to develop the ability to see as many words as possible at a single glance, only one phrase should show at a time; the phrases need not necessarily relate to each other.

Do-It-Yourself Games

1. Dominoes can be played with word cards instead of the usual dots. The student must match words instead of dots. This will provide practice in reading and matching words, as well as in discrimination between words that he may substitute for each other.

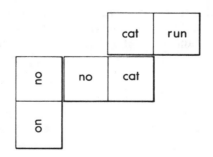

2. Making small words out of larger ones: Have the student make as many words as he can out of the letters in large words, such as **government: go, me, govern, men, never, ever, even, ten, move,** etc.

3. Decoding: Write simple sentences or stories for the student, omitting the vowels. Have the student complete the sentences: **Wh-n w-nt-r c-m-s, c-n spr-ng b- f-r b-h-nd?**

4. Rhymers. Encourage the student to think of words that rhyme. Prepare a set of puzzles similar to the following:

Think of **rode.**

heavy _____

like a frog_____

the lawn was _____

the seamstress _____

Think of **fate.**

At lunch she _____ .

The fence had a _____ .

The captain had a _____ .

Tardy means _____ .

Fish bite at _____ .

5. Editing. Have the student rewrite your stories, making corrections. In some, prepare silly errors. In others, have the student practice punctuation. For example, have the student write this story again. Tell him to put in 7 periods and 7 capital letters that are missing.

Ellen ran to school she went to the class the teacher was in the room the boys and girls were in their seats a cat was in the room it had no seat the teacher took lunch money from everyone the cat had no lunch money.

6. Hidden Words. Find the hidden words. Look for words, moving from left to right or from top to bottom. When you find a word, put an outline around it, and write it at the side of the page. Can you find nine words?

7. Buried Sentence. Move according to directions, and find the hidden sentence.

<pre>
s m l T a j z w
a t o h e e l x
c a n t h p e t
a t b e e h a n
</pre>

a. Start with T, down, right T _ _
b. Start with e, right, down, left, down, right, right, up.
     e _ _ _ _ _ _ _
c. Start with s, down, right. s _ _
d. Start with o, down. o _
e. Start with t, right, down. t _ _
f. Start with c, right, up. c _ _

T _ _ e _ _ _ _ _ _ _ s _ _ o _ t _ _ c _ _.

8. Anagrams, Bingo, Charades, Ghost, Geography, Lotto, Map Games, and Quiz Games are some common games that can very easily be adapted for reading instruction.

COMPANIES THAT MAKE GAMES

Antioch Bookplate Company, Yellow Springs, Ohio 45387

English Language Services, Inc., 800 18 Street NW, Washington, D.C. 20006

Exclusive Playing Card Company, 711 South Dearborn St., Chicago, Illinois 60605

Garrard Press, 1607 N. Market St., Champaign, Illinois 61820

Judy Company, 310 North Second Street, Minneapolis, Minnesota 55401

Kenworthy Programmed Teaching Aids, P.O. Box 3031, Buffalo, New York 14205

Kraeg Games, Inc., 4500 Shenandoah Avenue, St. Louis, Missouri 63110

Milton Bradley Company, Springfield, Massachusetts 01102

Parker Brothers, Inc., Salem, Massachusetts 01970

Remedial Education Center, 2138 Bancroft Place NW, Washington, D.C. 20008

Selchow and Righter Company, 200 Fifth Avenue, New York, N.Y. 10010

Helpful Publications

Materials Which Emphasize Word Analysis Skills,
Vocabulary Development, and Spelling

Column one lists the reading grade level of the material.
Column two indicates the age level of the students for whom the material will be interesting.

C	child, ages 6-11
ET	early teens, ages 12-15
YA	young adult
A	adult
All	all ages

	READING GRADE	INTEREST .LEVEL
A First Course In Phonic Reading, Helson, G., Educators Publishing Service	Beg.	All
A Second Course in Phonics, Helson, G. Educators Publishing Service	Beg.-3	ET, YA, A
Intersensory Reading Method, Pollack, C., Book-Lab, Inc.; unit designed to teach consonants and short vowels to non-readers.	Beg.	C, ET, YA
Learning the Letters, Educators Publishing Service	Beg.	C, ET, YA
Tutors Sampler, Pope, L., Edel, D., Haklay, A., Book Lab, Inc. Samples of materials and activities helpful in remedial reading instruction.	Beg.-3	A, All
Phonovisual Series, Phonovisual Products, Inc.	Beg.	C, ET
Phonics Is Fun, Modern Curriculum Press; A linguistic approach emphasizing early development of auditory skills. (Pace may be a little fast).	Beg.-3	C
MCP Basic Phonics Program; Modern Curriculum Press	Beg.-3	C

	READING GRADE	INTEREST LEVEL
Programmed Phonics Series, Educators Publishing Service; assumes a knowledge of consonant sounds.	Beg.	All
Specific Skill Series, Barnell Loft, Inc.; books A-F are at grade levels one through six; after the first level, the books may be used by students of any age as remedial workbooks for improving comprehension skills.	1-6	All
Reading With Phonics, J. B. Lippincott Company; accompanied by workbooks: *Sounds, Letters and Words; More Sounds, Letters and Words; Skill With Sounds.*	Beg.	C, ET
Structural Reading Series, Random House; useful for individual tutoring in early instruction.	Beg.	All
Conquests in Reading, Kottmeyer, W. and Ware, K., Webster Division, McGraw Hill Publishing Co.	Beg.-3	YA, A
McCall-Crabbs Standard Test Lessons in Reading, Teachers College Press.	2-12	All
Word Attack Series, Feldman, S. and Merrill, K., Teachers College Press; *Ways to Read Words* — Grade 2; *More Ways to Read Words* — Grade 3; *Learning About Words* — Grade 4.	2-4	All
Remedial Reading Drills, Hegge, T.G., and others, George Wahr Publishing Company.	Beg.-3	All
Phonics We Use, Lyons & Carnahan Educational Publishers; phonics exercises, with emphasis on auditory discrimination.	1-6	All
Thorndike-Barnhart Junior Dictionary, Doubleday and Company	4+	All
Mott Basic Language Skills Program, Allied Educational Council.	Beg.-3	ET, YA, A
Merrill Linguistic Readers, Charles E. Merrill Publishing Company; series with phonics approach.	Beg.-6	All
Let's Read, Clarence L. Barnhart Publishing Company.	1-3	C, ET, YA

168

	READING GRADE	INTEREST LEVEL
Open Court Correlated Language Arts Program, Open Court Publishing Company; basic readers, workbooks, and supplementary storybooks, stressing a phonics approach.	Beg.-6	C, ET
The Sullivan Associates Readers Series, McGraw-Hill Book Company; fourteen books stressing short vowels.	2-3	C
Basic Reading Series, McCracken, G. & Walcutt, C., J.B. Lippincott Company	Beg.-4	C, ET
Building Reading Skills, McCormick-Mathers Publishing Company.	Beg.-6	C, ET
Primary Phonics Series, Educators Publishing Service; brief pamphlet readers using consonants and short vowels, supplemented by workbook.	Beg.	C
Programmed Reading, McGraw-Hill Book Company.	1-3	C
Sullivan Reading Series, McGraw-Hill Book Company.	Beg.-3	C
First Phonics Series, Educators Publishing Service; introduction of consonants and short vowels, supplemented by consonant cards.	Beg.	C, ET
Stories to Accompany First Phonic Series, Educators Publishing Service.	Beg.	C, ET
Operation Alphabet, National Association of Public School Adult Educators; manual designed for use with television program of the same name.	Beg.-3	YA, A
Pacemaker Story Book, Grosher, G. R., Fearon Publishers.	2-3	YA, A
Programmed Reading for Adults Series, McGraw-Hill Book Company.	Beg.-5	YA, A
Word Power Made Easy, Lewis, N., Pocket Books.	9+	YA, A
Word Wealth, Miller, W., Holt, Rinehart & Winston.	9+	YA, A
Thirty Days to a More Powerful Vocabulary, Funk, W. & Lewis, N., Washington Square Press.	9+	YA, A
Arco High School Equivalency Book, Arco Publishing Company.	9+	YA, A

	READING GRADE	INTEREST LEVEL
Word Attack, Robert, Clyde, Harcourt, Brace & Janovitch, Inc.	7+	ET, YA, A
Vocabulary for College I and II, Diederick, P. & Carlton, S., Harcourt, Brace & World.	9+	YA, A
Thorndike-Barnhart High School Dictionary, Doubleday & Company.	9+	ET, YA, A
Modern Reading Skill Text, Book III, Charles E. Merrill Books, Inc.	9+	YA, A
English 2600, Harcourt, Brace & Janovitch	9+	YA, A
Mastering Good English, Continental Press.	9+	YA, A
Mastering Good Usage, Continental Press.	9+	YA, A
Practical English Workbook, Scholastic Book Service.	9+	YA, A
Essentials of Modern English, Pollack et al., Macmillan Company.	9+	YA, A
Hip Reader, Pollack & Lane, Book-Lab, Inc.; Two volumes.	1-3	ET, YA, A
New Streamlined English Series, Laubach, F. et al., New Readers Press; readers and skill books.	1-3	YA, A
Magnetic Patterns of the English Language, Baxter, W, Veritas Publications; an analytic approach to vocabulary, spelling and grammar.	4+	YA, A

Materials to Develop Comprehension and Encourage Interest and Pleasure in Reading

Gates Peardon Practice Exercises in Reading, Teachers College Press.	1-7	All
Readers' Choice Catalog, Scholastic Book Services; inexpensive paperback books.	2-12	All
Easy Reading Simplified Classics Series, Scott, Foresman & Company; popular titles include *Robinson Crusoe, Tom Sawyer, Moby Dick*.	3-5	All
Discovery Books, Garrard Publishing Company; popular titles include *Ulysses S. Grant, George Washington Carver, George Washington, Daniel Boone*.	3	All

	READING GRADE	INTEREST LEVEL
I Know a Place, Tannen, CSCS, Inc., a write it yourself book.	Beg.	All
True Books, Institutional Book Service.	1-2	All
New Practice Readers, Webster Division, McGraw-Hill Book Company; short selections.	2-4	
We Honor Them, Watson, W.M., New Readers Press; this two volume series presents easy to read one page biographies of important Negroes in American History.	2-4	All
Special Primary Series, Schwartz, L., Noble & Noble Publishers; five inexpensive workbooks designed for use with urban disadvantaged children, including supplementary units on preprimer level.	Beg.	C
Storybooks for Beginners, Fry, E., Dreier Educational System; an easy to read series.	Beg.	C
The Bank Street Readers, Macmillan Company; for urban disadvantaged children, including supplementary units on preprimer level.	Beg.-3	C
Dolch Series, Garrard Publishing Company; easy to read books using Dolch basic sight vocabulary.	1-3	C
Sailor Jack series, *Cowboy Sam* series, *Dan Frontier* and *Co-Basic Reading* series, Benefic Press.	Beg.-4	C
Morgan Bay Mystery series; Field Educational Publications.	2-4	C
The Moonbeam Books, Wasserman, S. and J., Benefic Press.	Beg.-5	C, ET
Jim Forest series, Harr Wagner Publishing Company.	1-3	C
Language Experience Readers (Chandler Reading Program) Chandler Publishing Company; the program includes paperback picture portfolios, preprimer paperback readers.	Beg.-3	C

	READING GRADE	INTEREST LEVEL
Holt Urban Social Studies Series, Holt, Rinehart & Winston, Inc.; attractively illustrated series.	2-4	C
The City Is My Home Series, John Day Company.	Beg.	C
Giant Step Storybooks, Readers Digest; Brief pamphlet readers using consonants and short vowels.	Beg.	C
Look, Read, Learn Books, Melmont Publishers; titles include *At the Airport, Freight Yard.*	2-3	C, ET
The Box Car Children Series, Scott, Foresman & Company.	2-5	C, ET
Reading Round Table Series, American Book Company.	1-6	C, ET
Adventures in Space Series. Fearon Publisher, Lear Siegler, Inc. Education Division.	1-3	C, ET
Cornerstone Readers, Field Educational Publications.	2-5	C, ET
Yearling Books, Dell Publishing Company; inexpensive paperback adaptations of children's classics include biographies of Frederick Douglass, Abraham Lincoln, and John F. Kennedy.	2-8	C, ET
Martin Mooney's Minute Mysteries, Educators Publishing Service; short stories.	3-4	C, ET, YA
Deep Sea Adventure Series, Field Educational Publications.	1-5	C, ET, YA
Cracking the Code, The Key to Independent Reading, Rasmussen and Goldberg. Science Research Associates.	Beg.-3	ET, YA, A
Checkered Flag Series, Field Education Publication.	2-3	C, Et, YA
Teen Age Tales, D. C. Heath & Company; short, interesting stories.	3-6	ET, YA
Breakthrough Series, Allyn and Bacon. Paperback readers with short stories of high interest level, especially appealing to urban minority groups.	3-5	ET, YA
Readers Digest Skill Builders, Readers Digest Services, Inc.	1-8	ET, YA

	READING GRADE	INTEREST LEVEL
Adult Reading Series, Readers Digest Services, Inc.; Twelve short reading booklets with comprehensive questions.	1-4	YA, A
New Rochester Occupational Reading Series: The Job Ahead, Science Research Associates; the same vocational material presented at each reading level.	2-5	YA, A
Accent Education Series, Follett Publishing Company. *You and They You are Heredity and Environment Taking Stock You and Your Needs You and Your Occupation Getting That Job*	3-4	YA, A
Reading for a Purpose, Follett Publishing Company; provides instruction at earliest reading level, including building of sight vocabulary.	Beg.	YA, A
Communications Series, Follett Publishing Company.	2-3	YA, A
Landmark Books, Random House; books of history and biography.	4-8	A
Macmillan Reading Spectrum, Macmillan Company; general instructional materials.	4-8	A
Individualized Reading Series, Meltzer, I. Book-Lab, Inc.; (titles include *Blacks in Early American History, Montgomery Bus Story, A School At Midnight, Black History; Events in February, Robert Smalls, Brave Seaman, Phyllis Wheatley, Young Poet, Frederick Douglass, Great Abolitionist, Harriet Tubman, Moses of Her People*).	4-6	ET, YA, A
Let's Talk About Drugs, Collins, C. et al, Book-Lab, Inc.; a reader and workbook describing the effects of drug abuse.	4-6	ET, YA, A
Citizens All Series, Houghton Mifflin Company; a series of social studies enrichment texts.	4-6	C, ET, YA

173

	READING GRADE	INTEREST LEVEL
Proudly We Hail, Brown, V. & Brown, J., Houghton Mifflin Company; brief illustrated biographies.	4-5	ET, YA
Holt's Impact Series, Holt, Rinehart & Winston; beautifully illustrated units; each unit contains anthology, record and ten paperback books.	6-9	ET, YA, A
Books for Reluctant Readers, Scholastic Book Services; inexpensive paperback readers.	5-8	ET, YA, A
Call Them Heroes, Silver-Burdett Company; a book of short biographies of minority group members.	5-6	ET, YA, A
The Getting Along Series, Frank E. Richards. *After School Is Out* *A Job at Last* *Money in the Pocket* *From Tires to Teeth*	5-6	YA
Vocational Reading Series, Follett Publishing Company. *Marie Perrone, Practical Nurse* *The Delso Sisters, Beauticians* *John Leverone, Auto Mechanic* *The Millers and Willie B. Butcher, Baker Chef*	4-6	ET, YA, A
Turner-Livingston Series, Follet Publishing Company. *The Money You Spend* *The Town You Live In* *The Jobs You Get* *The Person You Are* *The Friends You Make* *The Family You Belong To*	5-6	ET, YA, A
Turner-Livingston Series, Follett Publishing Company. *The Television You Watch* *The Phone Calls You Make* *The Newspaper You Read* *The Movies You See* *The Letters You Write* *The Language You Speak* *Understanding the Automobile*	6-7	ET, YA, A

	READING GRADE	INTEREST LEVEL
What Job for Me? Series, McGraw-Hill Book Company; eighteen pamphlet size paperback books providing vocational orientation; titles include *Carmen the Beautician, Nick the Waiter, Phil the File Clerk.*	4-6	YA
Reading for Meaning Series, J. B. Lippincott Company.	4-12	YA,
Falcon Books, Noble & Noble; especially adapted best sellers of high interest, easy reading levels, includes such titles as *Fail Safe, A Tree Grows in Brooklyn.*	4-12	YA, ET, A
Reading Development Kit, Addison Wesley Publishing Company; Kit A, second and third grade levels; Kit B, fourth to sixth grade levels; Kit C, seventh grade and above; the whole program requires minimum supervision.	2-9	YA, A
Macmillan Gateway Series, Macmillan Company anthologies.	7	YA, A
Reading Action Labs, Book-Lab, Inc.	3-4	C, ET

Games

(Generally Priced Under $5)

Alphabet, Childcraft.
ABC Game, Kenworthy Educational Service, Inc.
ABC Lotto, Childcraft.
Blend-O-Grams, Dorothea Alcock.
Consonant Lotto, Garrard Publishing Company.
Dog House Game, Beckley Cardy Company.
Easy Crossword Puzzles for People Learning English, Walter P. Allen, English Language Services.
Fun With Rhymes, Instructo Products Company.
Fun With Words, Dexter and Westbrook, Ltd.
Go Fish, A Consonant Blend Game, Remedial Education Center.
Go Fish, A Consonant Sound Game, Remedial Education Center.
Grab, (Deck 1, Deck 2, Senior), Dorothea Alcock.
Group Sounding Game, Garrard Publishing Company.
Group Word Teaching Game, Garrard Publishing Company.

Ideal Spellbinder Games, Ideal Toy Company:
   Space Flight, (game of blends)
   Zig Zag (game of rhyming words)
   Sea of Vowels (long and short vowel game)
   Silly Sounds (game of initial consonants)
Judy's Match-Ettes (for use at the reading-readiness level), Judy
   Company.
Junior Scrabble, Selchow and Righter Company.
Magic Squares Game Book, Sally Childs, Educators Publishing Service.
Match, Sets I and II, Garrard Publishing Company.
The Monkey Game, Dorothea Alcock.
My Puzzle Book, I, II, Garrard Publishing Company.
Object Lotto, Childcraft.
Pay the Cashier, Garrard Publishing Company.
Phonetic Quizmo, Milton Bradley Company.
Picture Dominoes, Childcraft.
Picture Readiness Game, Garrard Publishing Company.
Picture Word Builder, Milton Bradley Company.
Pirate Keys (for phonics instruction), Antioch Bookplate Company.
Read and Say (Verb Game), Garrard Publishing Company.
Rhyming Puzzle, Ideal Toy Company.
Riddle, Riddle Rhyme Time, Dexter and Westbrook, Ltd.
Rummy: Phonic Rummy; Junior Phonic Rummy, Phono Visual
   Products.
Scrabble, Selchow and Righter Company.
See and Say Puzzle Cards, Teaching Resources, Inc.
Sentence Builder, Milton Bradley Company.
Spill and Spell, Childcraft.
Show You Know, Then Go, Teaching Resources, Inc.
The Syllable Game, Garrard Publishing Company.
Thinker Puzzles, Academic Therapy Publications.
Take, Garrard Publishing Company.
Vowel Dominoes, Remedial Education Center.
Vowel Lotto, Garrard Publishing Company.
What the Letters Say, Garrard Publishing Company.
Who Gets It? Garrard Publishing Company.

Teaching Aids

(Priced under $6 except Aids Marked *)

Alpha Space Letters (rubber), Lauri Enterprises.
Alphabet Cards, Developmental Learning Materials.
Alphabet Sets, Creative Playthings.
Sight Words for the Seventies, Book-Lab Inc.

Consonant Blend Cards, Montessori Matters.
Digraphs, Montessori Matters.
Flannel Boards, Judy Manufacturing Company.
Groovy Letters, Ideal Toy Company.
Judy Alphabets, Judy Manufacturing Company.
Kinesthetic Alphabet Cards, Instructo Products Company.
Letter Blocks, (capitals/lower case), Childcraft.
Letter Form Board and Letters, Houghton Mifflin Company.
Long and Short Vowels, Instructo Products Company.
New Phonetic Word Drill Cards, Kenworthy Educational Service, Inc.
Opposite Concepts, Instructo Products Company.
Phonetic Word Blend Flip Charts, Kenworthy Educational Service,
    Inc.
Picture Word Cards, Garrard Publishing Company.
Pope Inventory of Basic Reading Skills, Book-Lab, Inc.
Popper Word Sets, Garrard Publishing Company.
Puppets, (animals, family), Creative Playthings.
Short Vowel Cards, Montessori Matters.
Short Vowel Drill, Remedial Education Center.
Sight Phrase Cards, Garrard Publishing Company.
Sight Words for the Seventies, Book-Lab, Inc.
Tablet Form Letter Paper, Montessori Matters.
Touch to Learn Beaded Letters, Childcraft.
Tutor's Sampler, Book-Lab, Inc.
Visual and Primary Tracking, Geake and Smith, Ann Arbor Press.
Vowel Wheels, Milton Bradley Company.
Word Prefixes, Kenworthy Educational Service, Inc.
Word Suffixes, Kenworthy Educational Service, Inc.

Periodicals

News For You (New Readers Press, Division of Laubach Literacy,
    1320 Jamesville Ave., Syracuse, New York 13210). Weekly news-
    paper in two levels of difficulty, of special interest to the young
    adult and adult reader; levels 3-4 and 5-6.
New York, New York, Random House, 201 E. 50th St., New York,
    New York 10022. Weekly newspaper published in five levels of
    difficulty.
Scope, Scholastic Magazines, Inc., 50 W. 44th Street, New York, New
    York 10036.
Popular Science, 355 Lexington Avenue, New York, New York 10017.
Popular Mechanics, 350 W. 55th Street, New York, New York 10019.
National Geographic Magazine, 17th and M Streets, NW, Washing-
    ton, D.C. 20036.

Natural History, American Museum of Natural History, 79th Street and Central Park West, New York, New York 10024.
Ebony, 1820 South Michigan Avenue, Chicago, Illinois 60616.
You and Your World, Xerox Education Publications, 245 Long Hill Road, Middletown, Conn. 06457.
Know Your World, Xerox Education Publications, 245 Long Hill Road, Middletown, Conn. 06457.
Weekly newspapers in two levels of difficulty
for slow readers of all ages.

Background Reading for the Tutor

Classroom Psychology, Ruth Fishtein; Book-Lab, Inc., 1973.
Culturally Deprived Child, Frank Riessman; Harper and Row, 1962
Education and Income, Patricia Sexton, Viking Press, 1961.
Effective Teaching of Reading, Albert J. Harris; David McKay Company, 1962.
Free and Inexpensive Educational Aids, Thos. J. Pepe; Dover Publishing Company, 1962.
Issues in Urban Education and Mental Health, Lillie Pope, Editor, Book-Lab, Inc., 1972.
Language and Learning Activities for the Disadvantaged Child, C. Bereiter and S. Engelmann, Anti-Defamation League of the B'nai B'rith.
Listening Aids Through the Grades, David Russell and Elizabeth F. Russell; Teachers College Press, 1959.
Primer for Parents, Paul McKee; Houghton Mifflin Co., 1966.
Reading Aids Through the Grades, David Russell and Etta Karp; Teachers College Press, 1951.
Slums and Suburbs, James Conant; McGraw-Hill Book Company, 1961.
Teacher, Sylvia Ashton-Warner, Simon and Schuster, Inc., (or Bantam Paperback), 1963.
Teacher's Guide for Remedial Reading, Wm. Kottmeyer; McGraw-Hill Book Company, 1958.
Teaching Reading to Adults, Edwin H. and Marie P. Smith; National Assoc. of Public School Adult Educators, 1962.
When You Teach English As A Second Language, Constance and Robert Jolly; Book-Lab, Inc., 1974.
You and Your Child's Reading, Charlotte Mergentime; Harcourt, Brace, and Janovitch, Inc., 1963.

178

Background Film for the Tutor

All For One: Tutorial Highlights, This film demonstrates an individual tutorial session. Psycho-Educational Center, Coney Island Hospital, Brooklyn, New York 11235.

Periodicals of Interest to the Tutor

Academic Therapy, 1539 Fourth Street, San Rafael, California 94901.
Day Care and Early Education, Behavioral Publications, 72 Fifth Avenue, New York, N.Y. 10011.
Early Years, Allen Raymond, Inc., Hale Lane, Darien, Conn. 06820.
Instructor, Instructor Publications, Inc., 7 Bank Street, Dansville, N.Y. 14437.
Journal of Reading, International Reading Association, 800 Barksdale Road, Newark, Delaware 19711.
Learning, 530 University Ave., Palo Alto, Calif. 94301.
Reading Teacher, International Reading Association, 800 Barksdale Road, Newark, Delaware 19711.
Teacher, Macmillan Professional Magazines, Inc., 22 West PUtnam Ave., Greenwich, Conn. 06830.
Teaching Exceptional Children, Council for Exceptional Children, 1920 Association Drive, Reston, Va. 22091.

Professional and Special Interest Associations

Alexander Graham Bell Association for the Deaf, 1537 - 35 St., N.W. Washington, D.C. 20007.
American Association on Mental Deficiency, 5201 Connecticut Ave., Washington, D.C. 20015.
American Federation of Teachers, 1012 14th St., N.W., Washington, D.C. 20005.
American Montessori Society, 175 Fifth Ave., New York, N.Y. 10010.
American Optometric Association, 7000 Chippewa St., St. Louis, Mo. 63119.
Association for the Aid of Crippled Children, 345 East 46 St., New York, N.Y. 10017.
Association for Children with Learning Disabilities, 5225 Grace St., Pittsburgh, Pa. 15236.
California Association for Neurologically Handicapped Children, 11291 MacNab St., Garden Grove, Calif. 92640.

Council for Exceptional Children, 1920 Association Dr., Reston, Va. 22091.

International Reading Association, 800 Barksdale Road, Newark, Delaware 19711.

National Association for Retarded Children, 420 Lexington Ave., New York, N.Y. 10017.

National Association for the Visually Handicapped, 305 E. 24 St., New York, N.Y. 10010.

National Education Association, 1201 16th St., N.W., Washington, D.C. 20036.

National Society for Crippled Children and Adults, 2023 West Ogden Ave., Chicago, Ill. 60600.

Orton Society, 8415 Bellona Lane, Towson, Md. 21204.

United Federation of Teachers, 260 Park Avenue South, New York, N.Y. 10003.

Directory of Publishers

Abelard-Schuman Limited, 257 Park Avenue South, New York, New York 10019.

Academic Therapy Publications, 1539 Fourth Street, San Rafael, California 94901.

Addison-Wesley Publishing Co., Inc., 2725 Sand Hill Road, Menlo Park, California 94025.

*Alcock, Dorothea, Covina, California 91722.

Allied Education Council, Distribution Center, Galien, Michigan 49113.

Allyn and Bacon, 470 Atlantic Avenue, Boston, Massachusetts 02210.

American Book Company, 450 W. 33rd Street, New York, New York 10003.

American Peoples Press, Inc., 155 North Wacker Drive, Chicago, Illinois 60606.

American Technical Society, 850 East 58th Street, Chicago, Illinois 60637.

American Textbook Publishers Institute, 432 Park Avenue, New York, New York 10016.

Ann Arbor Publishers, Box 1446, Ann Arbor, Michigan 48104.

Anti-Defamation League of B'nai B'rith, 315 Lexington Avenue, New York, New York 10036.

*Antioch Bookplate Company, Yellow Springs, Ohio 45387.

Arco Publishing Company, 219 Park Avenue South, New York, New York 10003.

Barnell Loft Ltd., 958 Church Street, Baldwin, New York 11510.

Barnhart, Clarence L., Box 359, Bronxville, New York 10708.

*Companies that make games.

180

Beckley-Cardy Company, 1900 North Narragansett Street, Chicago, Illinois 60639.

Bell and Howell Company, 7100 McCormick Road, Chicago, Illinois 60645.

Benefic Press, 10300 W. Roosevelt Road, Westchester, Illinois 60153.

Bobbs-Merrill Company, 4 W. 58th Street, New York, New York.

Book-Lab, Inc., 1449 - 37th Street, Brooklyn, New York 11218.

Bureau of Publications, Teachers College, Columbia University, New York, New York 10017.

*Cadaco-Ellis Company, 1446 Merchandise Mart, Chicago, Illinois 60654.

Chandler Publishing Company, 124 Spear Street, San Francisco, California 94105.

*Childcraft, 150 E. 58th Street, New York, New York 10022.

Children's Press, Inc., 1224 W. Van Buren Street, Chicago, Illinois 60607.

Cloidt, Gielow & Dudley, Inc., 175 W. Jackson Blvd., Chicago, Illinois 60604.

Compton, F. E., & Company, 425 N. Michigan Avenue, Chicago, Illinois 60611.

Continental Press, Elizabethtown, Pennsylvania 17022.

Coronet Instructional Media, 65 E. South Water Street, Chicago, Illinois 60601.

*Creative Playthings, Princeton, New Jersey 08540.

Thomas Y. Crowell Company, 666 Fifth Avenue, New York, New York 10019.

CSCS, Inc., Educational Publishers, 60 Commercial Wharf, Boston, Massachusetts.Dell Publishing Company, Inc., 1 Dag Hammar-skjold Plaza, New York, New York 10017.

Denoyer-Geppert Company, 5235 N. Ravenswood Avenue, Chicago, Illinois 60640.

*Developmental Learning Materials, 7440 Natchez Avenue, Niles, Illinois 60648.

Dexter and Westbrook, Ltd., Rockville Center, New York 11571.

Doubleday & Company, Institutional Department, Garden City, New York 11530.

Dover Publishing Company, 180 Varick Street, New York, New York 10014.

Dreier Educational Systems, 300 Raritan Ave., Highland Park, New Jersey 08904.

Educational Activities, 7937 Grand Avenue, Baldwin, New York 11510.

Educational Development Laboratories (Div. of McGraw-Hill), 1221 Avenue of the Americas, New York, New York 10020.

*Companies that make games.

181

Educator's Publishing Service, 75 Moulton Street, Cambridge, Massachusetts 02138.

Encyclopedia Britannica Educational Corp., 425 N. Michigan Avenue Chicago, Illinois 60611.

*English Language Services, Inc., 800 18th Street, NW, Washington, D.C.

*Exclusive Playing Card Company, 711 South Dearborn St., Chicago, Illinois 60605.

Fearon Publishers, 6 Davis Drive, Belmont, California 94002.

Ferguson Publishing Company, 6 N. Michigan Avenue, Chicago, Illinois 60602.

Field Educational Publications, 2400 Hanover Street, Palo Alto, California 94304.

Field Enterprises Educational Corp., 510 Merchandise Mart Plaza, Chicago, Illinois 60654.

Follett Publishing Company, 1010 W. Washington Street, Chicago, Illinois 60607.

*Garrard Publishing Company, 1607 N. Market Street, Champaigne, Illinois 61820.

Ginn & Company, 191 Spring Street, Lexington, Massachusetts 02173.

Hale, E.M., & Company, Eau Claire, Wisconsin 54701.

Hammond, C.S., & Company, 515 Valley Street, Maplewood, New Jersey 07040.

Harcourt Brace Jovanovich, Inc., 757 Third Avenue, New York, New York 10017.

Harper & Row Publishers, Inc., 2500 Crawford Avenue, Evanston, Illinois 60201.

Heath, D.C., & Company, 125 Spring Street, Lexington, Massachusetts 02173.

Holt, Rinehart & Winston, Inc., 383 Madison Avenue, New York, New York 10017.

*Houghton Mifflin Company, 1 Beacon Street, Boston, Massachusetts 02107.

Ideal School Supply Company, 11000 South Lavergne Avenue, Oak Lawn, Illinois 60453.

Institutional Book Service, 1224 W. Van Buren Street, Chicago, Illinois 60607.

*Instructo Products Co., Paoli, Pennsylvania 19301.

Instructor Magazine, 7 Bank Street, Danoville, New York 14437.

Irwin, Richard D., Inc., 1818 Ridge Road, Homewood, Illinois 60430.

John Day Company, Inc., 257 Park Avenue South, New York, New York 10010.

*Judy Company, 310 North Second Street, Minneapolis, Minnesota 55401.

*Companies that make games.

182

*Kenworthy Educational Service, Inc., P.O. Box 3031, Buffalo, New York 14205.

King Company, 2412 West Lawrence Avenue, Chicago, Illinois 60625.

*Kraeg Games, Inc., 4500 Shenandoah Avenue, St. Louis, Missouri 63110.

LaSalle Extension University, 417 S. Dearborn Street, Chicago, Illinois 60605.

Lippincott, J.B., Company, East Washington Square, Philadelphia, Pennsylvania 19105.

Loyola University Press, 3441 N. Ashland Avenue, Chicago, Illinois 60657.

Lyons & Carnahan Educational Publishers, 407 East 25th Street, Chicago, Illinois 60616.

McCormick-Mathers Publishing Company, 450 W. 33rd Street, New York, New York 10001.

McKay, David, 750 Third Avenue, New York, New York 10017.

Macmillan Company, 866 Third Avenue, New York, New York 10022.

Melmont Publishers, 1224 West Van Buren Street, Chicago, Illinois 60607.

Mentzer, Bush & Company, 645 N. Michigan Avenue, Chicago, Illinois 60611.

Merrill, Charles E., Books, Inc., 1300 Alum Creek Drive, Columbus, Ohio 43216.

*Milton Bradley Company, Springfield, Massachusetts 01102.

Modern Curriculum Press, 13900 Prospect Road, Cleveland, Ohio 44136.

Montessori Matters, Sisters of Notre Dame de Namur, 701 East Columbia Avenue, Cincinnati, Ohio 45215.

National Association of Public School Adult Educators, 1201 16th Street NW, Washington, D.C. 20006.

National Forum, 407 South Dearborn Street, Chicago, Illinois 60605.

National Textbook Corporation, 8259 Niles Center Road, Skokie, Illinois 60076.

New Readers Press, 1320 Jamesville Avenue, Syracuse, New York 13210.

New York University Press, 21 W. Fourth Street, New York, New York 10003.

Noble and Noble Publishers, 1 Dag Hammarskjold Plaza, New York, New York 10017.

O.A. Business Publications, Inc., 288 Park Avenue, Elmhurst, Illinois 60126.

Open Court Publishing Company, Box 599, LaSalle, Illinois 61301.

*Parker Brothers, Inc., Salem, Massachusetts 01970.

Phonovisual Products Inc., P.O. Box 5625, Washington, D.C. 20016.

*Companies that make games.

183

Pocket Books, Division of Simon and Schuster, Inc., 630 Fifth Avenue, New York, New York 10020.

Portal Press, Inc., 369 Lexington Avenue, New York, New York 10017.

Prentice-Hall, Inc., Educational Book Division, Englewood Cliffs, New Jersey 07632.

Putnam, G. P., Company, Inc., 200 Madison Avenue, New York, New York 10016.

Rand McNally & Company, P.O. Box 7600, Chicago, Illinois 60680.

Random House, 201 E. 50th Street, New York, New York 10022.

Reader's Digest Services, Educational Division, Pleasantville, New York 10570.

*Remedial Education Center, 2138 Bancroft Place NW, Washington, D.C. 20008.

Richards, Frank E., Publisher, 330 First Street, Liverpool, New York 13088.

Rowe, H.M., Company, 600 Van Buren Street, Chicago, Illinois 60607.

Scholastic Book Service, 50 W. 44th Street, New York, New York 10036.

Science Research Associates, Inc., 259 East Erie Street, Chicago, Illinois 60611.

Scott, Foresman & Company, 1900 E. Lake Drive, Chicago, Illinois 60611.

*Selchow and Righter Company, 200 Fifth Avenue, New York, New York 10010.

Silver Burdett Company, 250 James Street, Morristown, New Jersey 07960.

Simon & Schuster, Inc., 630 Fifth Avenue, New York, New York 10020.

Society for Visual Education, Inc., 1345 Diversey Parkway, Chicago, Illinois 60614.

South-Western Publishing Company, 5101 Madison Road, Cincinnati, Ohio 45227.

Speech and Language Materials, Inc., P.O. Box 721, Tulsa, Oklahoma 74101.

Standard Education Society, Inc., 130 North Wells Street, Chicago, Illinois 60606.

Steck-Vaughn Company, Box 2028, Austin, Texas 78767.

Summy-Birchard Publishing Company, 1834 Ridge Avenue, Evanston, Illinois 60201.

Teachers College Press, Teachers College, Columbia University, 1234 Amsterdam Avenue, New York, New York 10027.

Teachers Publishing Corporation, Box 2000, Darien, Connecticut 06820.

*Companies that make games.

184

*Teaching Resources, Inc., 100 Boylston Street, Boston, Massachusetts 02116.

United Educators, Inc., Tangley Oaks Educational Center, Lake Bluff, Illinois 60044.

United States Government Printing Office, Washington, D.C. 20025.

University of Chicago Press, 5801 South Ellis Avenue, Chicago, Illinois 60637.

Veritas Publications, P.O. Box 4085, Falls Church, Virginia 22044.

Viking Press, 625 Madison Avenue, New York, New York 10022.

Wahr, George, Publishing Company, Ann Arbor, Michigan.

Washington Square Press, Inc., 630 Fifth Avenue, New York, New York 10003.

Webster Division, McGraw-Hill Book Company, Manchester Road, Manchester, Missouri 63011.

Xerox Education Publications, 245 Long Hill Road, Middletown, Connecticut 06457.

* Companies that make games.

Glossary

accent: the stress given to a syllable so that it will be more prominent than other syllables; a characteristic pronunciation influenced by the speaker's native language or regional background.

affix: a prefix or suffix.

articulation: (in speech) the formation of speech sounds, the quality of clarity of speech sounds.

attention span: the length of time an individual can concentrate on simething without being distracted or losing interest.

auditory discrimination: the ability to hear and perceive differences between sounds that are similar, but not the same, as "p and b."

auditory perception: see auditory discrimination.

audiometer: an instrument used to test hearing.

basic education: a course of study in which the basic tools of reading, arithmetic, and writing are acquired; frequently applied to adult education classes.

blend: the fusion of two sounds smoothly, so that each one is heard separately; the fusion of several sounds to form a word.

compound word: a word that is made up of two or more words, such as baseball, firefly.

configuration clue: a clue based on the general shape of the word; recognizing the shape, the reader may read the word.

consonant: a letter that represents a speech sound produced by the closing or narrowing of the mouth or throat, as b, m, s.

consonant equivalents: the two or three possible sounds for the same consonant, as in s, c, g.

consonant blend: two or three consonants sounded together, in which each of the sounds is still heard distinctly, as "str" in street.

consonant digraph: a combination of two consonants producing a single sound. In some cases, one consonant of the combination is heard, as in **ck, kn, wr, gh, gn, wh**; in others, an entirely new sound is produced, as with **ch, th, sh, ph**.

context clues: clues used to figure out the pronunciation and meaning of an unfamiliar word through the meaning of known words in the sentence or paragraph surrounding it.

cursive writing: writing in which the letters are connected; usually called handwriting.

decoding approach: an approach to beginning reading instruction which emphasizes sounding out the written message. Phonics and linguistic methods both use a decoding approach.

derivative: a word composed of a root word plus a prefix or suffix.

developmental reading: reading instruction designed to teach the reading skills systematically. The term is usually applied to reading instruction for the new learner, as opposed to remedial reading instruction, which is for students who have failed to acquire the necessary skills in a developmental reading program.

diagnosis, reading: an analysis of a student's reading competence and the exact nature of his reading skills and deficits. Reading diagnosis also attempts to determine the cause of the reading disability, and to suggest remedial treatment.

diagnostic check-list: a list of skills involved in the process of reading, in which the student's skills and weakness are recorded.

diagnostic test: a test designed for and evaluating individual strengths and weaknesses in reading.

dialect: a special variety of a language in which the words, usage, and pronunciation are characteristic of specific localities.

digraph, consonant: see consonant digraph.

digraph, vowel: see vowel digraph.

diphthong, or vowel blend: a combination of two vowel sounds that blend to become one. Both sounds are blended together. The common vowel diphthongs are **oi, oy, ou, ow, ew**.

188

directional confusion: inability of the reader to move the eye consistently from left to right; this results in reversals in reading, for example, reading **was** for **saw.**

discrimination, auditory: see auditory discrimination

discrimination, word: the ability to distinguish one word for another.

dominance, lateral: the preference for use of one side of the body over the other, as preferring the right hand, the right eye, the right foot.

dyslexia: medical term for reading disability.

experience chart: a printed or handwritten chart recounting an experience of the student in the words of the student. Although the term chart is used because this is a tool traditionally used in classroom instruction, it is equally useful with the individual learner in remedial instruction.

expected grade placement: the grade in which students of the same chronological age are usually found. For example, expected grade placement for a six-year-old is first grade; for a fourteen-year-old, it is the ninth grade.

eye-span: the amount of written material that can be perceived by the eye in one fixation.

families, word: groups of rhyming words containing identical word elements. They are used in teaching word recognition. The student is drilled in those elements that are variable, as in **bat, hat, fat, cat, rat.**

flash cards: cards on which letters, words, or phrases are written or printed; they are used for rapid drill, in arithmetic as well as in reading instruction.

functional illiterate: the reader who reads below the fifth-grade level. In an industrial society, this reading level is inadequate for vocational competence in any occupations but those on the lowest economic level.

homograph: a word is spelled exactly the same as another, but is different in derivation and in meaning: as **sewer** (for waste disposal) and **sewer** (one who sews).

homonym: a word that sounds the same as another, but which differs in meaning and sometimes in spelling; as **to, too,** and **two.**

189

Idiom: an expression peculiar to a particular language.

Initial Teaching Alphabet (ITA): A 44-letter alphabet designed in England by Sir James Pitman to simplify the learning of reading. Each of the 44 letters in this alphabet stands for only one sound. Capital letters have the same shapes as small letters, instead of having different shapes, as do those in our alphabet.

instruction, individual: instruction given by a teacher to one person not in a group; tutoring.

instruction, individualized: each student's instruction is based on a careful assessment of his needs; each student, individually or in a group, usually proceeds at his own pace.

kinesthetic instruction: instruction making use of the muscle sense and muscle movement. In reading, the kinesthetic sense is involved when the student trace the outlines of letters and words.

linguistics: the science of language. A method of teaching reading that emphasizes a decoding, or sounding-out approach.

look-say method: the sight method, learning to recognize a word by its shape.

manuscript writing: writing by hand in a manner adapted from the printed letter; each letter is separately shaped, in contrast with cursive writing, in which the letters are joined.

method, experience: see experience chart.

method, kinesthetic: see kinesthetic instruction.

method, mirror: a method that involves using a mirror in which the reader reads the printed matter; this method is used for readers who make an extraordinary number of reversals.

method, phonic: teaching reading by associating the letters with the sounds they represent.

method, sight: teaching reading by having the reader respond to whole words rather than having him depend on the sounds of the letters.

method, whole word: see method, sight.

multisensory approach: an approach to teaching reading that makes use of all of the senses: visual (eyes), sight words; auditory (ears), phonic analysis; kinesthetic (sense of movement), tracing letters and words; tactile (touch), raised letters, sandpaper.

phoneme: a speech sound.

phonetic: the science of speech sounds.

190

phonics: the study of sound-letter relationships in reading and spelling.

phonogram: a letter or group of letters representing a speech sound.

picture clue: a picture illustrating written matter that provides a clue to word recognition and meaning.

prefix: a syllable added to the beginning of a word to modify its meaning.

readability: a measure of the reading difficulty of a passage, based on the length of sentence and the length and type of vocabulary.

reader, disabled: a reader whose level of reading competence is significantly lower than is expected of him.

reader, retarded: see reader, disabled.

reading level: the school grade is equivalent to the reading level for that grade.

reading readiness: the level of developmental maturity the child must reach before formal reading instruction will be effective. At this level, he is able to perceive similarities and differences in shapes, knows some of the letters, and probably already recognizes several words at sight.

reading, developmental: see developmental reading.

reading, remedial: see developmental reading.

reading, word-by-word: halting reading in which every word presents to the reader an obstacle that must be mastered before the next word is attacked.

reading level, frustration: the level at which reading skills are inadequate: the reading loses its fluency, and errors become more frequent than 5 in 100 words. The reader becomes tense and uncomfortable.

reading level, independent: the highest reading level at which one can read fluently and with a minimum of error without assistance.

reading level, instructional: the highest reading level at which one can read fluently under teacher supervision.

root word: the base word, from which words are developed by the addition of prefixes and suffixes, such as re **work, work** ing.

schwa: the soft sound for any vowel in an unstressed syllable, as **a** bout, penc **il**, lem **on**.

sight word: a word recognized by its shape.

structural analysis: analyzing a word by breaking it down into its parts (root, suffix, prefix); if it is a compound word, breaking it down into its component words.

scanning, or skimming: rapid reading to gain an overall impression, or to find specific information, overlooking details.

suffix: a letter or syllable added at the end of a word to modify its meaning.

syllable: a letter or group of letters representing a vowel sound; it may or may not contain one or more consonants.

syllabication: the process of dividing a word into single syllables.

synonym: a word whose meaning is similar to that of another word which is spelled and pronounced differently, as **large** and **big**.

tachistoscope: a device that exposes material for a brief period of time so that it must be read at a glance.

test, diagnostic: see diagnostic test.

tool subject: a subject involving the learning of a skill that is necessary for the learning of other subjects: reading, writing, arithmetic.

visual discrimination: the ability to distinguish likenesses and differences between shapes, particularly letters and words.

visual perception: see visual discrimination.

vowel: a letter representing a sound made with the mouth open. The vowel letters are **a, e, i, o, u.** Sometimes **y** is used as a vowel.

vowel digraph (or teams): combinations of two vowels, or a vowel followed by w, which represents a single speech sound: **ai, ea, ie, oa, ay, ea, oo, au, ei, ow, aw.**

word: a symbol of an idea; the smallest unit representing an idea.

word wheel: a device used to drill in word attack skills. It consists of two circular cards clipped together, each containing different word elements.

word attack skills: word analysis.

workbook: practice book, in which the student writes, that provides drill material in the reading skills. Workbooks sometimes accompany the textbook; at other times, they are prepared independently in order to provide practice in specific skill areas.

word family: see family, word.